DESCENT FROM PARNASSUS

DESCENT
from
PARNASSUS

---

by

DILYS POWELL

Essay Index Reprint Series

BOOKS FOR LIBRARIES PRESS
FREEPORT, NEW YORK

PR
610
.P6
1969

First Published 1935
Reprinted 1969

STANDARD BOOK NUMBER:
8369-1374-4

LIBRARY OF CONGRESS CATALOG CARD NUMBER:
75-99720

PRINTED IN THE UNITED STATES OF AMERICA

THIS BOOK IS DEDICATED TO
THE MEMORY OF MY FATHER
THOMAS POWELL

CONTENTS

FOREWORD

It is no longer reasonable to deny that the form of poetry is changing ; what ten or twenty years ago seemed eccentricity is now shown to be an importunate poetic impulse. There are, of course, verse-writers who use the elasticity of the new forms to disguise insensibility to form of any kind. But poetry emerges from the chaos of experiment ; and to reject the new movements altogether, preferring the attempt to rejuvenate the old, is to fail in the receptivity which is part of the critic's equipment. It is to fail in distinguishing between the genuine and the manufactured in poetry ; in short, to betray the whole profession of criticism.

The following essays deal with the work of poets who have been instrumental in bringing about the change. Not all can still be regarded as innovators. Miss Sitwell, for instance, has done her pioneering, and we are now able to regard her work, not as controversy, but as poetry. The fact remains that she was one of the writers who bridged the gap between the sterile years of the early war and the post-war years of excited experiment ; that she helped to keep the interest in poetry alive when it was near extinction.

We are not far enough away in time from the first stages of innovation to make an historical judgement. But it is not too soon to trace a direction ; nor is it unimportant, to those who care for poetry (they are not many), to pause at this stage and ask where it is leading us.

The change in form has been of two main kinds. Firstly, of course, there has been the tendency towards obscurity. Poetry has been growing more and more difficult to understand ; sometimes it has required a violent intellectual effort, sometimes unusual knowledge ; sometimes, leaping the bounds of the logical altogether, it has become rationally incomprehensible. There has, in fact, been a sudden movement away from the common reader. Obviously before we can appreciate poetry we must know what it is about. The inclination of much critical writing has been to evade this part of the problem, and straightway to tackle the more advanced and more spectacular question of form. But no solution of the second problem is possible unless it is based on a solution of the first ; least of all now, when much poetry opposes to the reader so thick a veil of obscurity. I have therefore concerned myself in these essays firstly with subject matter, and where meaning, in the sense of a logical sequence of ideas, has seemed absent, I have tried to show what significance can be implicit in the apparently irrational.

The second change in form has been in the opposite direction—towards a greater simplicity. But not the

Georgian simplicity of what Mr. Sherard Vines calls a " cosy, home-made art " ; rather a simplicity produced by a contempt for art. We find at one end of the scale the genius of Lawrence abandoning itself to the barest doggerel ; at the other, the talent of Mr. Sassoon is angered into colloquialism and slang. In both cases it is a deliberate rejection of the conventionally " poetic " ; once more the common reader is rebuffed, this time not by any logical difficulty, but by the absence of the graces he has learned to expect. In both cases it is not so much technical experiment as the expression of a moral point of view with which we have to deal. Mr. Sassoon's plain and rather gawky style has had only an indirect influence in breaking down a poetic convention. But Lawrence's truculent jingles have had a direct effect on verse ; and among the younger writers there is an increasing desire to compose poetry out of flat statement. Experiment, in fact, is still going on ; and in the last of these essays I have discussed the work of three members of the new advance guard.

In attempting to elucidate the themes of serious poetry we find something approaching a common mood. Lawrence, Mr. Eliot and Miss Sitwell, however different their approach, all express this mood ; so, in lesser degree, does Mr. Sassoon. In addition, then, to illustrating a period of experiment and innovation in English poetry, the writers here treated represent a psychological phase. I have emphasized the psychological problem because it seems to me essential to an under-

standing of the poetry, if understanding is to be anything more than a facile acceptance of inconsistencies
and enigmas. For in psychology we find not only an
explanation of theme, but also a clue to its treatment.
Obviously it is vital to remember what some critics
forget, that it is with literature, not pathology, that
we are dealing. But if psychology, instead of being
allowed to enslave criticism, is harnessed to it, the critic
has a powerful ally: an ally capable of helping him
to illuminate one of the main problems, that of the
relation between meaning and form.

With each writer I have tried to disentangle the
central conflict. Mr. Charles Williams in his interesting study " The English Poetic Mind " declares the
work of Shakespeare, Milton and Wordsworth to be
rooted in conflict between the ideal and the actual :
" this is, and is not, Cressid." [1] Certainly most
modern poetry is motivated by conflict : discrepancy
between the writer's temperament and his convictions,
between his experience and his belief. When, however, we come to the new generation, to the work of
Mr. Auden, Mr. Day Lewis, Mr. Spender, the nature
of the conflict has changed. It has been externalized ;
it has become a battle, not within the poet, but between
poetry and environment. And the mood has suffered
a violent reversal. The new verse has ceased to doubt
and look back ; it has begun to hope and look forward.
To what extent the reader, too, may look forward is
doubtful. Some people, indeed, have allowed them-

[1] " Troilus and Cressida," Act V, Scene 2, 143.

selves to wonder whether poetry as we know it will survive its conflict with environment. The one thing certain is that we have reached a crucial point. It is from that point that I have attempted to survey the immediate past of poetry and to give some idea of the mixture of promise and menace which is the present.

D. H. LAWRENCE

D. H. LAWRENCE

D. H. Lawrence is best known as a novelist ; rightly, because it is for his narrative and descriptive prose that he will ultimately be remembered. But his poetry has its importance. It is important intrinsically, since it is the poetry of a genius. And it is important in relation to the prose. The novels, beginning as scarcely disguised autobiography, become as time goes on more and more the expression of a creed : a creed illumined by magnificent character-drawing and set against a stupendous natural background, but still a creed. Unlike Mr. Shaw's plays, Lawrence's novels have no prefaces. But the poetry with its direct expression of the momentary mood, and its simple statement of ideas complicated in the prose by the reactions of the characters, provides the perfect commentary. I shall try to show how the psychology of the verse clarifies the psychology of the prose fiction. But it is impossible to judge the commentary without first looking at the text ; let me then begin by giving a slight indication of the general purport of the novels.

Lawrence's first novel (and first published book), "The White Peacock", appeared in 1911. It is the

story of a young farmer who, refused by a clever
" spiritual " woman, marries a barmaid and drinks
himself rotten. The following year came " The Trespasser ". Here the man is a musician who hopes to find
in a mistress an escape from his mean suburban life ;
the woman (another deep " interesting " creature)
accepts him, but reluctantly and even with distaste,
and a conviction that he has failed as a lover drives
him to suicide. The year 1913 gave us " Sons and
Lovers "—the childhood and youth of a miner's son,
his first unsatisfactory love-affair with a girl who dreads
physical intercourse, and the death of the mother on
whom his life has been pivoted. The spiritual woman
is a recurring character ; in the later books the spirituality diminishes, but it is still there. She is the serpent
in Lawrence's sexual Eden ; luring others to destruction, she is herself her own Hell. For Lawrence the
woman who would save her soul must first lose it. The
heroine of " The Lost Girl " (1920) endures a middle-
class girlhood impeccable save for a short interval as a
nurse, when, suddenly grown strapping and vulgar,
she indulges in some scuffles with amorous doctors.
" Sometimes her blood really came up in the fight,
and she felt as if, with her hands, she could tear any
man, any male creature, limb from limb. A superhuman, voltaic force filled her. For a moment she
surged in massive, inhuman, female strength. The
men always wilted." Then she falls in love with an
Italian circus performer and goes to live with him in
a cranny of the Alban Hills where she is indeed " lost ".

4

Of the three women beatified in " The Ladybird "
(1923), the first becomes the mistress of an undersized
Count who promises her a share of his throne in Hades ;
the second renounces the dubious independence of
poultry-farming to sink her consciousness in life with
a self-willed boy ; the third commits herself to hon-
ouring and obeying a lover who does not want and
does not offer love. The scintillating widow whose
part in the establishment of a new religion in Mexico
is the subject of " The Plumed Serpent " (1926) ends
by marrying an Indian with whom she lives in " a
mindless communion of the blood ". And in " The
Woman Who Rode Away " (1928) out it comes again—
" the one enduring thing a woman can have, the
intangible soft flood of contentment that carries her
along at the side of the man she is married to. It is
her perfection and her highest attainment."

Sex and the achievement of a just balance between
man's physical domination and woman's physical
mutiny—this appears to be the central problem of
Lawrence's prose fiction. One or two other themes
recur. The story of " The White Peacock " is told by
the farmer's friend—a bookish young man whose slight
physique contrasts with the " white fruitfulness " of
the other ; the two suitors of " Women in Love "
(1921) supply the same physical contrast and feel the
same physical attraction. And in " Aaron's Rod "
(1922) and " Kangaroo " (1923) Lawrence is still trying to conceive a relation between men which shall
supplement the relation between men and women.

5

Sometimes a character's career is followed in a second novel ; Ursula of " The Rainbow " (1915) is Ursula of " Women in Love " ; sometimes characters reappear under different names : George and Emily of " The White Peacock " are easily recognized in Edgar and Miriam of " Sons and Lovers ". Autobiographical incidents are obvious in the early novels ; in " The White Peacock " with its rural landscapes and its pictures of exile in a London suburb, shadowed by the Crystal Palace " pricking up its two round towers like pillars of anxious misery " ; in " Sons and Lovers " with its superb descriptions of a mining village. But in the later novels autobiography is often displaced by dogma, though Lawrence is still drawing on his personal experience. He has set the burden of recollection down on paper ; having won certain convictions, he is free to give them expression ; and so we come to the mystical doctrines of " The Plumed Serpent "— its sexual symbolism, its rejection of the " spiritual " founder of Christianity, and its return to an older, physical race of gods with the male strength of the sun and the female strength of the earth. It is Lawrence's single way to salvation. " Man is a mistake, he must go," he makes a character say in " Women in Love " ; but apparently there is a chance of man's being allowed to stay if he returns to his true sensuality, " the dark involuntary being ". Lacking this, civilization must destroy itself.

We have, then, a prose writer who attaches an enormous importance to the sensual life ; who hates with a hatred which is both moral and physical the self-conscious, asensual civilization of the twentieth century. He has been called the Carlyle of this generation. The critic faced with the magnificent outbursts of grief and anger, contempt and despair which go to make up the work of Lawrence may well feel that he has to deal, not with the Carlyle, but with the Jeremiah of our day.

. . . .

The poems may be divided roughly into four sections. There are the " Rhyming Poems " which, taken from " Love Poems and Others " (1913), " Amores " (1916), " New Poems " (1918), and " Bay " (1919), make up the first volume of the " Collected Poems " and cover much the same ground as the first three novels, " The White Peacock ", " The Trespasser " and " Sons and Lovers ". These comprise rural poems, love poems, poems to his mother, dialect poems, war poems and a few poems about school and London. Next there is the autobiographical cycle " Look ! We Have Come Through ! " (1917), a collection of poems " intended as an essential story, or history, or confession, unfolding one from the other in organic development, the whole revealing the intrinsic experience of a man during the crisis of manhood, when he marries and comes into himself ". Lawrence with his customary candour supplies the argument. " After much struggling and loss in love and in the world of man, the protagonist throws in his lot with a woman who is already married. Together they go into another country, she perforce leaving her children behind. The conflict of love and hate goes on between the man and the woman, and between these two and the world around them, till it reaches some sort of conclusion." Thirdly there is the collection " Birds, Beasts and Flowers " (1923), in which, as in the later novels, autobiography gives way to dogma. These poems, descriptive and rhetorical pieces about trees and their fruits, about animals and birds and reptiles, are only superficially objective ; Lawrence finds tongues in trees, takes the tortoise as the text of a sermon on sex, and sees in the overripe fig the symbol of the modern woman. Finally we have " Pansies " (1929), so called " because they are rather ' Pensées ' than anything else "—" merely the breath of the moment, and one eternal moment easily contradicting the next eternal moment " ; the posthumous " Nettles " (1930), a group of doggerel satires on English prudery and servility; and "Last Poems " (1932), which adds further momentary reflections to the existing " Pansies " and shows Lawrence faced with the problem of death and dissolution.

It is clear that as time goes on he becomes less and less subject to the conventions of form and matter. " A young man ", he says in the " Note " to his " Collected Poems " (1928, 2 vols.), " is afraid of his demon and puts his hand over the demon's mouth sometimes and speaks for him. And the things the young man says are very rarely poetry." Later on the demon was released. " I have tried to let the demon say his say, and to remove the passages where the young man intruded. So that, in the first volume, many poems are changed, some entirely rewritten, recast. But usually this is only because the poem started out to be something which it didn't quite achieve, because the young man interfered with his demon." Lawrence is in fact concerned to remove every barrier to his own subjective truth. But the interesting thing is his explicit statement that his poems make up " a biography of an emotional and inner life ". For this reason he arranged them as far as possible in chronological order. " The poems to Miriam, and to my Mother, and to Helen, and to the other woman, the woman of ' Kisses in the Train ' and ' Hands of the Betrothed ', they need the order of time, as that is the order of experience. So, perhaps, do the subjective poems like ' Virgin Youth '." Lawrence goes on to inform his readers that at the age of twenty-three he left Nottinghamshire to teach in a school on the fringes of London (" then the poems to Helen begin, and the school poems, and London ") ; that the death of his mother " with the long haunting of death in life " is the crisis of Volume I ; that in 1912 he left England for the first time and in the same year began the cycle " Look ! We Have Come Through ! " (published in 1917) which opens with " Bei Hennef ", written by a river in the Rhineland, and ends with " Frost Flowers ", written in Cornwall at the end of the bitter winter of 1916–17. " It seems to me ", he adds, " that no poetry, not even the best, should be judged as if it existed in the absolute, in the vacuum

9

of the absolute. . . . If we knew a little more of Shakespeare's self and circumstance how much more complete the Sonnets would be to us, how their strange, torn edges would be softened and merged into a whole body ! So one would like to ask the reader of ' Look ! We Have Come Through ! ' to fill in the background of the poems, as far as possible, with the place, the time, the circumstance. What was uttered in the cruel spring of 1917 should not be dislocated and heard as if sounding out of the void." We must, in fact, beware of taking every line as a final truth about its author ; and we need not attempt to reconcile every pair of the contradictions which are inevitable in the work of a man so bent on confession.

One of the first things we notice in the rhyming poems is the intensity of their physical feeling. Lawrence's nature poetry has none of the deliberate observation which characterizes Georgian nature poetry or the poetry of the beginning of the Romantic movement ; it is the record, not of carefully noted impressions, but of vivid experience. His effects are obtained with a curious contempt for detail ; we look in vain for the catalogues of birds and flowers which commonly decorate descriptions of landscape. His knowledge of the countryside goes too deep for detail ; he is himself too vitally involved in nature to be able to observe it with the detachment of the artist. As a rule the poet aware of this profound sympathy with non-human life translates it into terms of mental and spiritual activity : the Romantics of the beginning of the nineteenth century,

for instance, are constantly impelled by it into emotional
exploration and philosophical speculation. Lawrence
in his earlier verse keeps to the physical plane ; his
rural poems express sharp personal sensation, or if
there is a translation it is into terms of something
stronger than sensation, into terms of passion.

Look now, through the woods where the beech-green spurts
Like a storm of emerald snow, now see !
A great bay stallion dances, skirts
    The bushes sumptuously,
Going out in spring to the round of his tame deserts.

And you, my lass, with your rich warm face aglow,
What sudden expectation opens you
So wide as you watch the catkins blow
    Their dust from the birch on the blue
Life of the pulsing wind ? ah, say that you know !

Like most poets, in fact, he uses his intimacy with
nature to give form to immediate preoccupations ; and
these, with him, are physical.

The natural background of the early poems is the
perfect sympathetic accompaniment to the autobiography which these make up ; the whole landscape is
convulsed with his desires, with his sufferings and his
ecstasies. And against this background of valleys

        Fleshed all like me
    With feelings that change and quiver
    And clash, and yet seem to tally,

of scented night and moonrise

            . . . like a breast revealed
        By the slipping shawl of stars.—

of orchard " where violets secretly darken the earth "
and flaunting common where

> The quick sparks on the gorse-bushes are leaping,
> Little jets of sunlight texture imitating flame ;

is unfolded the story of a troubled childhood and a
tormented youth. The story is, as I have said, known
to us from " Sons and Lovers " and to a lesser degree
from " The White Peacock " and " The Trespasser " ;
here it is inevitably less complete. But it is as if certain
episodes in the prose had been picked out by a spot-
light ; the result is not a connected drama, but a series
of crucial moments illuminated by brilliant and pitiless
self-examination. In this series of flashes we see the
collier's home in the Midlands where Lawrence lived
as a child, with the wind in the ash-tree outside mimick-
ing the discord between man and wife in the house ;
we see the heartrending interdependence of mother and
son and the young man's breaking away ; we see the
mother's death and the son's ineffable bereavement.

> Nay, but she sleeps like a bride, and dreams her dreams
> > Of perfect things.
> She lies at last, the darling, in the shape of her dream,
> > And her dead mouth sings
> By its shape, like thrushes in clear evenings.

All these poems to his mother show an exquisite and
agonizing tenderness ; English verse has nothing better
of its kind. But before the death the scene has changed.
The young man has gone to London, and we see his

reactions to the first contact with a great city and his
struggles and disappointments as a teacher ; and later
we see his bitterness and shame during the War.   But
meanwhile another theme has appeared : the search
for " some condition of blessedness " amidst the conflict of sex.   At first it runs parallel to the record of
other experiences ; later it overwhelms everything else.
To the end of his life this problem will be immensely
important to him.   For the present it is crystallized in
three episodes—the episode of Miriam, the country
girl of " Sons and Lovers "—

> You only endured, and it broke
> My craftsman's nerve.
> No flesh responded to my stroke ;
> So I failed to give you the last
> Fine torture you did deserve.—

the episode of Helen, the woman of " The Trespasser " :

I in the fur of the world, alone ; but this Helen close by !
How we hate one another to-night, hate, she and I
To numbness and nothingness ; I dead, she refusing to die.
The female whose venom can more than kill, can numb and
 then nullify.—

the episode of the third, unnamed woman :

> So she came down from above
> And emptied my heart of love.
> So I held my heart aloft
> To the cuckoo that hung like a dove,
> And she settled soft.—

which one may assume is continued in " Look !   We

Have Come Through ! " where the conflict between man and woman is brought to " some sort of conclusion ". The Miriam and Helen episodes are not merely inconclusive : they are catastrophic. In both cases the young man meets a woman whose physical coldness humiliates his sexual pride. In the first she is generous against her instinct and her will ; in the second her submission is malignant ; she is the type " with whom the dream was always more than the reality ", and who for centuries " has been rejecting the ' animal ' in humanity, till now her dreams are abstract, and full of fantasy, and her blood runs in bondage, and her kindness is full of cruelty ". Both episodes are significant, since in them is the beginning of the fanatical hatred of the " spiritual " and the " intellectual " woman which characterizes all Lawrence's subsequent writings. They gave, in fact, a peculiar bias to his views on women ; but it is important to recognize that they were not responsible for his emphasis on the problem of sex. The physical quality which marks his style and which we see in his nature poetry is enough to prove that emphasis to be the expression of an original inclination. A man whose physical preoccupations were less insistent might have been persuaded by the ignominious failure of his first attempts at solution to put aside the whole problem. Failure and humiliation merely further convinced Lawrence of its pivotal place in life.

But before he enunciates a creed he must solve his personal problem ; he must be tried in conflict with a single woman. In the first section of the " unrhym-

14

ing " poems, " Look ! We Have Come Through ! "
(published before the later of the rhyming poems), the
field has narrowed down to an intersexual duel without
seconds. The sense of frustration which pervades the
rhyming poems has vanished ; in its place there is
tension and torment, though with halcyon moments of
repose. We are given the history of the struggle for a
complete understanding, once more in a series of
flashes : the flashes faithfully represent the violent
reversals of feeling natural to a passionate relationship
of this kind. We see the rebound from the cynicism of
" Loggerheads " :

> If despair is our portion
> Then let us despair.
> Let us make for the weeping willow.
> I don't care.—

to the tenderness of " Valentine's Night " :

> My love, my blossom, a child
> Almost ! The flower in the bud
> Again, undefiled.
>
> And yet, a woman, knowing
> All, good, evil, both
> In one blossom blowing.

We are made witnesses of the man's terror of separation
and his humiliating dependence on the woman :

> God, that I have no choice !
> That my own fulfilment is up against me
> Timelessly !
> The burden of self-accomplishment !

> The charge of fulfilment !
> And God, that she is *necessary* !
> *Necessary*, and I have no choice !—

and in contrast we watch his moods of masculine self-assertion and his vision of a mutual independence :

> Since you are confined in the orbit of me
> do you not loathe the confinement ?
> Is not even the beauty and peace of an orbit
> an intolerable prison to you,
> as it is to everybody ?
>
> But we will learn to submit
> each of us to the balanced, eternal orbit
> wherein we circle on our fate
> in strange conjunction.

Gradually we realize that this mutual independence is the goal towards which he is struggling. To Lawrence, for the perfect sexual relationship love is not enough. Love implies possession and domination and a diminution of freedom, and thence proceeds hatred : a stage must be reached beyond love and hate. There is a stage, he says, where the self dies and is born again. Beyond abandonment to the sexual ecstasy lies fulfilment ; and in fulfilment the self is extinguished, yet, perishing, recognizes the co-existence of the other being, the woman.

> Plunging as I have done, over the brink
> I have dropped at last headlong into nought, plunging upon
>   sheer hard extinction ;
> I have come, as it were, not to know,
> died, as it were ; ceased from knowing ; surpassed myself.
> What can I say more, except that I know what it is to surpass
>   myself ?

It is a kind of death which is not death.
It is going a little beyond the bounds.
How can one speak, where there is a dumbness on one's
    mouth ?
I suppose, ultimately she is all beyond me,
she is all not-me, ultimately.
It is that that one comes to.
A curious agony, and a relief, when I touch that which is
    not me in any sense,
it wounds me to death with my own not-being ; definite,
    inviolable limitation,
and something beyond, quite beyond, if you understand what
    that means.
It is the major part of being, this having surpassed oneself,
this having touched the edge of the beyond, and perished,
    yet not perished.

By recognition of the other being, the self is kindled to
new life, and the man and the woman, the self and
the not-self, achieve existence in equilibrium but separate ; and therein is freedom.

It is in pure, unutterable resolvedness, distinction of being,
    that one is free,
not in mixing, merging, not in similarity.

But in the perfect relationship the woman too must
recognize the not-self, the man.

then I shall be glad, I shall not be confused with her,
I shall be cleared, distinct, single as if burnished in silver,
having no adherence, no adhesion anywhere,
one clear, burnished, isolated being, unique,
and she also, pure, isolated, complete,
two of us, unutterably distinguished, and in unutterable conjunction.

And Lawrence looks into the future towards an age when " all men detach themselves and become unique " and we shall move in freedom " conditioned only by our own pure single being ".

Mr. Middleton Murry has been at pains to explain the important poem from which the last three passages are taken,[1]—and indeed the whole sequence of poems —as evidence of Lawrence's excessive dependence on the woman. " If he knows himself as isolated and unique, with a true and certain knowledge, what does it matter to him whether the woman recognizes him as isolated and unique ? " [2] The unprejudiced mind will understand that the emphasis on distinction, on the isolation of self from not-self, comes of that desire for individuality which sets men above the animals— and which Lawrence was not the first to express. What is distinct in his treatment of the problem of identity is his approach through sex. Sex for him becomes the means not only to the reassertion of the body against the pretensions of the spirit, but also to a state of developed consciousness ; it is not surprising that he should think it vitally important. Obviously, unless the woman is able to share the ultra-physical as well as the physical experience, the sexual relationship is im-perfect. But at least Lawrence has come in sight of the perfect relationship. He may hereafter seem to have lost it from view ; he may forget that in his original conception the woman too must have her

[1] " Manifesto."
[2] " Son of Woman," p. 110 (Cape).

18

" isolated being " ; for the moment he has seen a solution of his difficulties.

In " Manifesto " Lawrence formulates his Athanasian creed : the two in one, the one in two. " Birds, Beasts and Flowers ", the second section of the " un-rhyming " poems (which, it may be noted, often rhyme), shows him again concerned with duality ; but there has been a move from particular to general. It is no longer a question of establishing harmonious relations between a single man and a single woman ; Lawrence uses the birds and beasts and flowers he describes to symbolize the problems of all men and all women. Even the harmless tortoise stands for the duality of sex :

His adolescence saw him crucified into sex,
Doomed, in the long crucifixion of desire, to seek his consummation beyond himself.
Divided into passionate duality,

and for its reintegration :

Torn, to become whole again, after long seeking for what is lost,
The same cry from the tortoise as from Christ, the Osiris-cry of abandonment,
That which is whole, torn asunder,
That which is in part, finding its whole again throughout the universe.

But Lawrence is now beginning to generalize about another kind of dualism : the division of man between spirit and flesh. In the rhyming poems he was occupied in a personal quarrel with over-emphasis on the

spiritual ; now he makes even the evangelist Matthew
protest against the " wings of the spirit " :

So I will be lifted up, Saviour,
But put me down again in time, Master,
Before my heart stops beating, and I become what I am not.
Put me down again on the earth, Jesus, on the brown soil
Where flowers sprout in the acrid humus, and fade into humus
    again.
Where beasts drop their unlicked young, and pasture, and
    drop their droppings among the turf.
Where the adder darts horizontal.
Down on the damp, unceasing ground, where my feet belong
And even my heart, Lord, forever, after all uplifting :
The crumbling, damp, fresh land, life horizontal and ceaseless.

Gradually " spirituality " is identified with Christianity,
whose founder he begins to hold responsible for humanity's lost balance. And in opposition he exalts the
qualities which Christianity rejects.

There is only one evil, to deny life

he writes, and calls for the destruction and rebirth of
society :

But not a trace of foul equality,
Nor sound of still more foul human perfection.

Above all he insists on the virtues of the flesh. The
physical feeling which is present in his earliest poems
becomes in " Birds, Beasts and Flowers " overpowering ;
and more and more the emphasis is laid not merely
on the physical, but on the sexual. A ripe fig, a pack-
ass, a field of anemones, each is capable of provoking

20

a tirade on sex—on sex the balance of which is being
destroyed by woman's rejection of her true rights in
favour of a false independence.   His struggles for personal " blessedness " have made him acutely sensitive
to discord in others ; feeling excessively, he charges
with his sensibility even the most customary phenomena.   The poetry which results is often magnificent ;
it is also often oppressive.   The symbolism appears too
heavy for its object ; even the turkey's wattles

> (Turkey-cock, turkey-cock,
> Are you the bird of the next dawn ?)

are " The overdrip of a great passion hanging in the
balance ".   This is not simply the poet transforming
the commonplace by his superior imagination : it is
the poet plagued by emotions which exceed the normal
means of expression.   Lawrence's anger and disgust at
the degradation in which he sees society involved,
sharpened by personal animosity, demand continual
outlet.   And their importunacy becomes so tormenting
that he tries to escape, not only by expressing them, but
also by imagining a society in which they would be
quieted.   We must go back, he says, to a subtler,
non-mental state of consciousness, back across

> . . . the fern-scented frontiers
> Of the world before the floods, where man was dark and
>   evasive
> And the tiny vine-flower rose of all roses, perfumed,
> And all in naked communion communicating as now our
>   clothed vision can never communicate.

Or we must recapture " the delicate magic of life "
which was lost when the Etruscans vanished, or the
" sinister splendour " of the " sombre, dead, feather-
lustrous Aztecs " ; or perhaps we may even go forward
and find in America

The new Proud Republic
Based on the mystery of pride.
Overweening men, full of power of life, commanding a teem-
ing obedience.

Ultimately, of course, it is not only a decaying civilization from which we have to escape : we have also to
escape from Lawrence's own agonizing sensibilities.   Not
surprising that no permanently satisfactory refuge offers
itself ; not surprising that even in New Mexico there is

A dark membrane over the will, holding a man down
Even when the mind has flickered awake ;
A membrane of sleep, like a black blanket.

The victory of " Look ! We Have Come Through ! ",
then, was not final, since it left Lawrence still at war
with society.   In " Pansies " and " Nettles " the warfare has become guerrilla.   Lawrence has retreated into
the fastnesses of his own bitter resignation, though from
time to time he sallies out against the bourgeois " like
a fungus, living on the remains of bygone life ", or
against democracy and " the culture bait ", against
humility or caution or hypocrisy ; it is noticeable that
when he does so his anger and contempt find relief in
verse which is no more than doggerel.   Faithfully he
records every flicker of a restless imagination.   But on

two themes his mind is fixed. It is fixed in its hatred
of a mechanical civilization based on money (" our
madness, our vast collective madness ") and run by
" corpse-anatomies with ready-made sensations ! " ;
and it is fixed in its emphasis on the present-day misuse
of sex. Love has become " mind-perverted, will-per-
verted, ego-perverted " ; we have sex in the mind, but
none in the body. True sex is " a state of grace ".
There is a universal rhythm, a life-flow

Out of the soul's middle to the middle-most sun, way-off,
   or in every atom.

Sex is an essential part of this universal flow ; and in
disturbing the sexual rhythm we are disturbing the
universal rhythm. Ultimately, we see, the two themes
are the same : civilization is mechanical because it is
" cerebral ", " ego-bound ", because it has subjected
the body to the mind.

   But the moods of contempt and hatred alternate with
moods of indifference or passive waiting ; moods in
which Lawrence feels that for humanity at large " our
day is over ", that we are doomed to annihilation,

   . . . gone like weed, like weed, like eggs of fishes,
like sperm of whales, like germs of the great dead past
into which the creative future shall blow strange, unknown
   forms ?

and for himself

      I cannot help but be alone
      for desire has died in me, silence has grown,
      and nothing now reaches out to draw
      other flesh to my own.

Nothing now remains but " to die the amazing death ",
the death of our era.

And yet, as we die, why should not our vast mechanized day
    die with us,
so that when we are re-born, we can be born into a fresh world.

For the new word is Resurrection.

We must, in fact, die that we may be born again ; born
again in " the resurrection of the flesh ".

It is from this point that the posthumous " Last
Poems " continues. The volume repeats many of the
themes of " Pansies ". It recognizes a will to evil in
the world, manifest in the domination of man by
machines and in the self-absorption of the ego. It
appeals for human relations based, not on the emotions,
but on " the mystery of touch ". It affirms the essential
inequality of mankind and the division into slaves and
freemen, " machine-spawn " and " men of the vivid
life ". And here comes the crux ; to Lawrence it is
organic connection with " the living cosmos " which
distinguishes freeman from slave. The slave, the robot,
is the " ego-centric self "—

the ego running in its own complex and disconnected notion—

he is the wheel which, turning on itself, ignores all
other movement. The cosmos is " wandering " ; life
is " a wandering, we know not wither, but going " ;
only the ego, spinning on itself, is severed from the
universal flow.

The universe, then, has its being in movement, in

progress ; the machine is evil, the enemy of life, because
it is static. A curious group of mythological poems,
embodying the symbolism of the prose work on Revelation, " Apocalypse " (1932), insists on the principle of
conflict too : " Life is for kissing and for horrid strife ".
With perpetual opposition of delight and dread, love
and hate, heaven and hell, the creation goes its wandering path. And as it moves it enacts the threefold cycle
of death and re-birth. Eras are born, come to maturity
and decay. " What was a creative god, Ouranos,
Kronos, becomes at the end of the time-period a des-
troyer and a devourer," says Lawrence in " Apocalypse ". In " Last Poems " he repeats his conviction
that a new age is at hand, that the era of the Logos is
at an end :

. . . the foot of the Cross no longer is planted in the place of
the birth of the Sun.

and that the " spiritual " consciousness which it engendered has become the enemy of life.

Within the cycle of " time-periods ", the cycle of
" the tree of life ". The ceaseless flow of energy
between the cosmos and the individual is nourished by
death, the " long process of disintegration " which, as
with a fallen leaf,

can melt the detached life back
through the dark Hades at the roots of the tree
into the circulating sap, once more, of the tree of life.

Finally the cycle of the individual life, moving through
death to rebirth and renewal :

25

I shall blossom like a dark pansy, and be delighted
there among the dark sun-rays of death.
I can feel myself unfolding in the dark sunshine of death
to something flowery and fulfilled, and with a strange sweet
    perfume.

Lawrence's own approach to that " dark sunshine "
gives the death poems a terrible poignancy. But we
must not be misled by the tragedy which overhung
him into supposing that all these poems deal with
physical dissolution. Many are, indeed, concerned
with bodily death and

    . . . the core of dark and absolute
    oblivion where the soul at last is lost
    in utter peace.

—peace from which it emerges " new-created ". But
he is thinking, too, of the mystic death

    that lies between the old self and the new.

And, harking back again and again to the symbolism
of the pagan death-ritual described in " Apocalypse ",
he tells us that man, if he is to survive, must " suffer a
sense-change " ; he must be

resurrected from the death of mechanical motion and
    emotion.

—he must learn to explore

    . . . vast realms of consciousness still undreamed of.

For

    No man, unless he has died, and learnt to be alone
    will ever come into touch.

Even in life we must pass through the waters of oblivion and be born again. But if we cling to our old selves the very universe grows inimical. The pagan world believed that the dead, the superseded, were always dangerous. The sun and moon, says " Apocalypse ", in so far as they are old and superseded, are hostile to the old self, the old flesh of man ; and so

> when the daytime consciousness has got overweening
> when thoughts are stiff, like old leaves
> and ideas are hard, like acorns ready to fall.

even the brilliance of day strangles " the issues of our soul ". And Lawrence, pursuing the pagan idea, urges pity and propitiation of the dead who were thrust unprepared out of life.

Perhaps even now you are suffering from the havoc they make unknown within your breast and your deadened loins.

Physical death, just as much as the mystic death, must be a surrender to the universal flow. It is the false independence of the spirit which puts the time out of joint.

. . . . . .

The prose and the poetry, we have seen, often cover the same ground in Lawrence's life ; it is interesting to compare the two versions of an incident or a scene.

There is in " The White Peacock " a description of a walk on the Embankment at night ; the narrator and his friend see the outcasts under Waterloo Bridge, give money to a sleeping woman, and hurry away

through the rain. Two poems reproduce the scene.
" All the faces were covered but two," says the prose,
" that of a peaked, pale little man, and that of a brutal
woman. Over these two faces, floating like uneasy
pale dreams on their obscurity, swept now and again
the trailing light of the tram cars." Here is the
verse :

> Two naked faces are seen
> Bare and asleep,
> Two pale clots swept by the light of the cars.
> Foam-clots showing between
> The long, low tidal-heap,
> The mud-weed opening two pale, shadowless stars.

> Over the pallor of only two faces
> Passes the gallivant beam of the trams ;
> Shows in only two sad places
> The white bare bone of our shams.

> A little, bearded man, peaked in sleeping,
> With a face like a chickweed flower.
> And a heavy woman, sleeping still keeping
> Callous and dour.

> Over the pallor of only two places
> Tossed on the low, black, ruffled heap
> Passes the light of the tram as it races
> Out of the deep.

Again, of the sleeping woman, the prose says : " Her
hands were pushed in the bosom of her jacket. She
lurched forward in her sleep, started, and one of her
hands fell out of her bosom. She sank again to sleep.
George gripped my arm.

" ' Give her something,' he whispered in panic. I was afraid. Then suddenly getting a florin from my pocket, I stiffened my nerves and slid it into her palm. Her hand was soft, and warm, and curled in sleep. She started violently, looking up at me, then down at her hand. I turned my face aside, terrified lest she should look in my eyes, and full of shame and grief I ran down the embankment to him."

This is the verse :

By the river
In the black wet night as the furtive rain slinks down,
Dropping and starting from sleep
Alone on a seat
A woman crouches.

I must go back to her.

I want to give her
Some money. Her hand slips out of the breast of her gown
Asleep. My fingers creep
Carefully over the sweet
Thumb-mound, into the palm's deep pouches.

So the gift !

God, how she starts !
And looks at me, and looks in the palm of her hand
And again at me !—
I turn and run
Down the Embankment, run for my life.

We must remember that we are dealing here with the earliest prose and with poetry, too, of an early period ; but I think that as a general rule the relation between these two versions stands. Lawrence is forced by the exigencies of rhyme and metre into an elaboration wanting in the prose ; compare the " peaked, pale little man " with the

> . . . little, bearded man, peaked in sleeping,
> With a face like a chickweed flowei.

And such concessions as he makes to poetic diction blunt the edges of his phrases ; what a difference in sharpness between " Her hand was soft, and warm, and curled in sleep " and

> . . . over the sweet
> Thumb-mound, into the palm's deep pouches.— !

The truth is that Lawrence feels himself hampered by verse technique ; it is partly for this reason that as he grows more sure of himself he adopts free verse (and with Lawrence it really is free), and towards the end of his life slips contemptuously into doggerel. The earlier, rhyming poems are themselves undisciplined, And when, as in the case of " The Wild Common ", or " Virgin Youth ", he later rewrites earlier poems, the second version shows no great tightening of discipline. " They were struggling ", he writes of the first versions, " to say something which it takes a man twenty years to be able to say." The emphasis is not on technique but on subjective truth. In " The Wild Common " he is developing his favourite theme, the dependence of " insolent soul " on " supple body " ; here is part of the first version :

So my soul like a passionate woman turns,
Filled with remorseful terror to the man she scorned, and her
    love
For myself in my own eyes' laughter burns,
Runs ecstatic over the pliant folds rippling down to my belly
    from the breast-lights above.

Over my sunlit skin the warm, clinging air,
Rich with the song of seven larks singing at once, goes kissing
    me glad.
And the soul of the wind and my blood compare
Their wandering happiness, and the wind, wasted in liberty,
    drifts on and is sad.

Oh but the water loves me and folds me,
Plays with me, sways me, lifts me and sinks me as though
    it were living blood,
Blood of a heaving woman who holds me up,
Owning my supple body a rare glad thing, supremely good.

Here is the second :

But how splendid it is to be substance, here !
My shadow is neither here nor there ; but I, I am royally
    here !
I am here ! I am here ! screams the peewit ; the may-blobs
    burst out in a laugh as they hear !
Here ! flick the rabbits. Here ! pants the gorse. Here !
    say the insects far and near.

Over my skin in the sunshine, the warm, clinging air
Flushed with the song of seven larks singing at once, goes
    kissing me glad.
You are here ! You are here ! We have found you ! Every-
    where
We sought you substantial, you touchstone of caresses, you
    naked lad !

Oh but the water loves me and folds me,
Plays with me, sways me, lifts me and sinks me, murmurs :
   Oh marvellous stuff !
No longer shadow !—and it holds me
Close, and it rolls me, enfolds me, touches me, as if never it
   could touch me enough.

Twenty years have taught Lawrence, it seems, not to
discipline his verse, but to take greater liberties with
it, to reject literary phrases and to use colloquialisms
in their place. The movement of the poem has become
quicker and more violent. But more important than
technical differences is the heightening of sensation :
" to be substance, here ! " ; " touchstone of caresses " ;
" as if never it could touch me enough ". Up to the
publication in 1923 of " Birds, Beasts and Flowers ",
the development of Lawrence's style is in the direction
of an intenser physical effect. The rhyming poems
with their uneven, carelessly voluptuous rhythms are
full of sensual colours and images : the "white-bodied"
night, the " bud-like blossoming of passion ", the red
hawthorn

     Like flags in pale blood newly wet,

the " pageant of flowery trees . . . pale-passionate ",
silence pouring

Through invisible pulses, slowly, filling the night's dark vein,

the moon rising " divesting herself of her golden shift ",
a woman's room

    . . . where the night still hangs like a half-folded bat,
And passion unbearable seethes in the darkness, like must
   in a vat.

Darkness itself—the " concrete darkness ", the " dark's deep fallow ", the " shut lips of the darkness ", the " rocking darkness ", the " fleece of night "—becomes tangible and sensuous, the challenge of passionate flesh to the soft spiritual light of the moon

> Frail as a scar upon the pale blue sky,

the moon " worn and frayed with cold ", " wistful and candid "—

> . . . the first white love of my youth, passionless and in vain.

But the death of Lawrence's mother chilled much of the earlier verse ; and in " Look ! We Have Come Through ! " he still feels the stream of his life.

> . . . in the darkness
> Deathward set !

It is only towards the end of the cycle that life reclaims him completely—and that the style of his poetry responds. While he is occupied with his own sexual problem his style, too, is turned inwards upon itself. Love and hate, fulfilment and unfulfilment, harmony and confusion, equilibrium and recoil, isolation and conjunction, annihilation and resurrection : the repetitive vocabulary echoes the minutely circling thought. Lawrence is getting rid of the bonds of rhyme and metre ; but not until he sees a solution to his personal problem and redeems the failure of the early episodes is he quite sure of himself. The close of " Look ! We Have Come Through ! " gives a promise of self-con-

fidence. But only with " Birds, Beasts and Flowers "
does physical rapture come to its full blossoming.
Suddenly we are aware of a developed, violently
individual style. The epithets break out into extravagant splendour : " the many-cicatrized frail vine ",
" spontaneous aconite, Hell-glamorous ", " sinuous,
flame-tall cypresses ", " the rare and orchid-like Evil-
yclept Etruscans ", the " Jaguar-splashed, puma-yellow,
leopard-livid slopes of America ". Almond blossom is
" sword-blade-born ", a fish's eye " red-gold, water-
precious, mirror-flat " ; crocuses are " stripe-cheeked
whelps, whippet-slim " ; infernal Dis is " flower-
sumptuous-blooded " ; the cyclamen puts out leaves

> Toad-filmy, earth-iridescent
> Beautiful
> Frost-filigreed
> Spumed with mud
> Snail-nacreous

Repetition is a vital element in this developed style ;
repetition with variations. When the almond tree puts
out its " flakes of rose-pale snow ", says Lawrence, it
is as if we were to see " rusty iron puff with clouds of
blossom ".

Iron, dawn-hearted,
Ever-beating dawn-heart, enveloped in iron against the
    exile, against the ages.

See it come forth in blossom
From the snow-remembering heart
In long-nighted January,
In the long dark nights of the evening star, and Sirius, and the
    Etna snow-wind through the long night.

Sweating his drops of blood through the long-nighted Gethsemane
Into blossom, into pride, into honey-triumph, into most
exquisite splendour.

Immediately the themes—iron, snow, wind, night, star,
heart, Gethsemane,—are repeated :

Something must be reassuring to the almond, in the evening
star, and the snow-wind, and the long, long nights,

So that the faith in his heart smiles again

And the Gethsemane blood at the iron pores unfolds, unfolds,

Then a new theme is introduced :

A naked tree of blossom, like a bridegroom bathing in dew,
divested of cover,
Frail-naked, utterly uncovered
To the green night-baying of the dog-star, Etna's snow-edged
wind
And January's loud-seeming sun.—

which, repeated, enriches the earlier themes :

Think of it, from the iron fastness
Suddenly to dare to come out naked, in perfection of blossom,
beyond the sword-rust.
Think, to stand there in full-unfolded nudity, smiling,
With all the snow-wind, and the sun-glare, and the dog-star
baying epithalamion.

" Iron ", " blossom ", " sword-rust ", " full-unfolded ",
" nudity ", " smiling ", " snow-wind ", " sun-glare ",
" dog-star ", " epithalamion ",—every phrase, every

image holds an echo of what has gone before. To the end of this magnificent poem the themes balance and interweave. " Honey-bodied ", " fragile-tender " " dawn-tender ", " more fearless than iron ", " subtly-smiling assurance ", " sword-blade-born ", " sore-hearted " : it is the contrapuntal method in poetry. We see that in spite of the careless unpolished rhythms of the verse Lawrence does not altogether disregard the problems of construction.

Together with the tropical vocabulary and the hammer-beat repetitions appears a new sharpness of image. The snake flickers his tongue " like a forked night on the air " ; the bat, " a black glove thrown up at the light ", loops between day and night " with spools of dark thread sewing the shadows together " ; the Mediterranean cyclamens spring up between the stones

> Arching
> Waking, pricking their ears
> Like delicate very-young greyhound bitches
> Half-yawning at the open, inexperienced
> Vista of day,
> Folding back their soundless petalled ears.

It is a sharpness proceeding from physical apprehension ; I have already said that the physical element in Lawrence's poetry at this period is overwhelming not only by its reminders of " the dark blood " and " the crucifixion of desire " and " the female mystery, covert and inward ", but also by its intensification of natural objects ; even the salvia is

36

The anger-reddened, golden-throated salvia
With its long antennæ of rage put out
Upon the frightened air.

Sometimes it becomes frankly brutal, sometimes even
sadistic :

It must be you who desire
this intermingling of the black and monstrous fingers of Moloch
in the blood-jets of your throat.—

Thus he addresses the " Rabbit Snared in the Night "
of " Look ! We Have Come Through ! " A fineness
in him has been blunted ; a delicacy which we sometimes see, in the early poems, suffering or affronted has
been so often outraged that it has turned to cruelty.
It is perhaps only to be expected that the arrival at
physical and mental assurance should be accompanied
by a certain coarsening of the sensibilities. And with
assurance comes, too, the indifference to conventional
forms which we see in the " unrhyming " poems.
Lawrence is no longer hampered by verse technique ;
he triumphs by ignoring it.

After " Birds, Beasts and Flowers " there is an interval
of six years ; by the time " Pansies " appears there has
been a great change in style. The volume has two
moods : the mood of resignation, the mood of contempt. The latter is expressed, as I have said, in doggerel. There are, it is true, flashes of the old magnifi-
cence ; but for the most part Lawrence is too much
exhausted by anger and disgust to be capable of the
physical explosions of " Birds, Beasts and Flowers ".

Instead, there are jets of coarseness ; there are insolent colloquialisms :

> Once and for all, have done with it,
> all the silly bunk
> of upper-class superiority ; that superior
> stuff is just holy skunk.

And suddenly the verse will break out in a doggerel cackle :

> Stand up, but not for Jesus !
> It's a little late for that.
> Stand up for justice and a jolly life.
> I'll hold your hat.

A large proportion of " Pansies " is written in doggerel rhyme—I think because the writer was too tired any longer to generate spontaneous rhythms. The feeling of the whole book is tired. Lawrence is worn out by psychological generosity :

> I have given myself to the people when they came
> so cultured, even bringing little gifts,
> so they pecked a shred of my life, and flew off with a croak
> of sneaking exultance.—

and by physical generosity :

> I have no desire any more
> towards woman or man, bird, beast or creature or thing.

When he is not writing doggerel the movement of the verse echoes a mood of resignation and indifference. The repetition no longer has a hammer-beat urgency :

The feelings I don't have I don't have.
The feelings I don't have, I won't say I have.
The feelings you say you have, you don't have.

—this is only tired insistence. The cadences are
cadences of exhaustion :

> Even the old emotions are finished,
> We have worn them out.
> And desire is dead.
> And the end of all things is inside us.

Often the lines become so inert that they slip into
prose, disguised or undisguised. Only now and then
there is a stirring of life, a gentleness delivered, like the
Risen Lord of the poem and the story, from death
itself :

> Desire may be dead
> and still a man can be
> a meeting place for sun and rain,
> wonder outwaiting pain
> as in a wintry tree.

The posthumous volume " Last Poems " (which we
must remember was not revised for publication) is
compiled from two manuscripts, one of which, called
by the editor " More Pansies ", is for the most part
a recapitulation of the book discussed above. There
are the same doggerel outbursts ; there is the same
sagging into prose ; the vocabulary is as impatient of
poetic conventions. Abstract terms are common—
universalism, cosmopolitanism, democracy, variegation,

nonentity, anarchy. The verse is ratiocinative instead of impulsive ; Lawrence admonishes where he once proclaimed :

> You are like to die of malnutrition of the senses :
> and your sensual atrophy
> will at last send you insane.

Sometimes we even meet an aphorism :

> The profound sensual experience of truth : Yea, this *is* !
> alone satisfies us, in the end.

Occasionally physical alertness returns, but in general there is a desire to evade the physical ; the sensitiveness which once responded to every contact now shrinks away, crying

> . . . to be alone, to possess one's soul in silence.

—Lawrence is not only tired, he is bruised and sore.

But from soreness is born the gentleness which we noticed struggling to be delivered in " Pansies " ; and in the second manuscript of " Last Poems " there is a release of tenderness and delicacy. The vocabulary admits in profusion soft darkling words—oblivion, peace, death, silence, ocean, flood. The unrhymed verse moves smoothly as if borne on a tideless sea.

> Now it is autumn and the falling fruit
> and the long journey towards oblivion.

> The apples falling like great drops of dew
> to bruise themselves an exit from themselves.

And it is time to go, to bid farewell
to one's own self, and find an exit
from the fallen self.

The querulousness of " Pansies " has disappeared ;
quiet broods over this final poetry.

And if, as autumn deepens and darkens
I feel the pain of falling leaves, and stems that break in storms
and trouble and dissolution and distress
and then the softness of deep shadows folding, folding
around my soul and spirit, around my lips
so sweet, like a swoon, or more like the drowse of a low, sad
 song
singing darker than the nightingale, on, on to the solstice
and the silence of short days, the silence of the year, the
 shadow,
then I shall know that my life is moving still
with the dark earth, and drenched
with the deep oblivion of earth's lapse and renewal.

At last Lawrence is tired unto death. But after death
comes rebirth. There is in these "Last Poems" an
actual return of physical awareness ; once more he
proclaims that " the rainbow has a body ", that " the
redness of a red geranium " is " a sensual experience ".
Again he delights in contrast—

> a thing of kisses and strife
> a lit-up shaft of rain
> a calling column of blood
> a rose tree bronzey with thorns

He responds again to the excitement of the pagan
world—or rather his idea of the pagan world. And
the symbolism which he finds in the Apocalypse sup-

plies him with a new flashing imagery—" the Dividers, the Thunderers, the Swift Ones ", " the angels of the Kiss ", " the Four Roots ". But there is more than this. The death-feeling which hovers over " Pansies " and " More Pansies " has suffered in " Last Poems " a metamorphosis into life ; it has been defeated by the idea of resurrection. However autumnal the mode, from time to time the verse puts out a daring blossom :

Reach me a gentian, give me a torch !
let me guide myself with the blue, forked torch of this flower
down the darker and darker stairs, where blue is darkened
    on blueness
even where Persephone goes, just now, from the frosted
    September
to the sightless realm where darkness is awake upon the dark
and Persephone herself is but a voice
or a darkness invisible enfolded in the deeper dark
of the arms Plutonic, and pierced with the passion of dense
    gloom,
among the splendour of torches of darkness, shedding dark-
    ness on the lost bride and her groom.

The nether world harbours that passion in which is life everlasting ; the grave itself becomes the nuptial bed.

Lawrence's verse describes in its progress from birth to death a curve which follows the parabola of the life of man. The early poems are ardent, sensitive, uncertain ; they are passionate but incomplete ; their physical quality is intense but fitful, vaguely directed. Next comes the conflict ; the poetry, like the man, is struggling for completeness, for constancy to itself and

stability in face of a hostile world. There is a brief
period of triumph. The man's physical powers are at
their height ; he is equal to society. And in sympathy
the poetry bursts out in magnificent bravado. Lawrence's real interests are moral. But for a time physical
exuberance forces him to submerge his moral interests.
He loads the simplest theme with extravagant decoration ; the verse breaks out into loops, into patterns,
into arabesques. Then the decline ; vitality ebbs
away, and with it the capacity for decoration. The
moral interests rise to the surface once more. " Desire
is dead ", mourns Lawrence—and drops into prose.
Without the stimulus of physical passion he cannot
write poetry ; he merely makes moral statements. (It
is perhaps for the same reason that "Lady Chatterley's
Lover " is an artistic failure ; he wrote it too late.)
Only when death has opened the door to resurrection,
only when dead desire has made way for a new and
living tenderness, to a quiet recognition of the universal
rhythm, does he again produce genuine poetry. Then,
indeed, the assurance of life everlasting and the consciousness of participation in the universal flow urge
him to a poetry based not on passion but on the knowledge of passion. But it is important to realize that,
up to the surrender to the mystic death, his poetry is
rooted in the physical. Its best period.coincides with
his period of greatest physical assurance ; its worst with
his period of physical torpor. When desire fails he can
write only doggerel.

. . . .

43

I have tried in this essay to confine myself to a consideration of the poetry, referring to the prose only for comparison and not for explanation. And it seems to me that in the poetry alone we can find a fairly complete record of Lawrence's emotional experiences and of their hardening into doctrine. Indeed, poetry being as a rule more immediate than prose, more spontaneous and less complicated by after-thoughts, it is likely to provide us with a more truthful record ; the narrative may be sketchier, but it is in essentials more reliable. Lawrence's poems have great intrinsic value ; they also perform an important function. They interpret the obscurities of the novels ; their frank self-revelation dispels the uncertainties and reconciles the contradictions of the prose. Novelists often superimpose decorative poetry on the fabric of their work ; Lawrence's poetry, standing out against the background of the novels, gives rather the clue to their intricate pattern. It is not a decoration, but a document.

What, then, does this document show us ? It shows us first of all the " prophet " on whom so much ill-informed criticism has been focused. Lawrence, growing up in a collier's family amidst the poverty of a mining district, soon becomes aware that something is wrong with civilization. The struggles and torments of his early manhood deepen the impression. The War, having aroused in him all the fury of the reformer, drives him to frenzy by proving him helpless ; he feels himself " dead, and trodden to nought in the smoke-sodden tomb ". After the War he looks about him and

sees a " dust-heap ", a " stinking rubbish-heap ", a
" glutted squirming populousness " ; in the midst of
a world to whose natural beauties he is acutely sensitive,
he is conscious that only man is ignoble. Civilization
is a failure ; and Lawrence is not the first to cry Woe !

His instinct is, of course, like Jonah to take to flight
—to Sicily, to Sardinia, to Australia, to New Mexico
—or, if needs be, out of life altogether, to the dead
world of the Etruscans, the Aztecs. But always, as one
pursued, he turns at bay ; he shouts back imprecations,
warnings, prophecies. We have mechanized life itself,
he cries. Man alone on earth is damned because he
has cut himself off from the living cosmos, which is
God. We must at all costs recover the lost connection ;
we must get back into " touch ". (Let me say once
and for all that this desire to regain " touch " explains
all his supposed retrograde movements.) But how are
we to get back ? Prophets are usually ready enough
with their advice but reticent as to the means of following it ; Lawrence is little more explicit than the rest.
We must, he says, obey our deepest consciousness ; we
must seek " the sheer coition of the life-flow " and

> Contact with the sun of suns
> that shines somewhere in the atom,

And, somehow, we may achieve salvation through sex.
Man has too long worshipped Christ and the spirit ;
let him now remember the body. Sex is a means to
contact with the universal flow ; it is also, as we have
seen, a means to the individuality, the singleness of

45

being without which man destroys himself. Sometimes it is a crucifixion, sometimes " a kind of death which is not death " ; but still a crucifixion, a death on the way to blessedness. It is never simply a pleasure ; Lawrence is by upbringing a Puritan, and even sex must be put to use as a moral instrument. And in the final instance he subordinates the human relationship to the universal rhythm ; essentially a religious man, he subjects human love to awe of God—a " dark God ". Even in " Kangaroo ", which is often regarded as the expression of all that was most undisciplined and dangerous in Lawrence, he says : " The only thing is the God who is the source of all passion. Once go down before the God-passion and human passions take their right rhythm. But human love without the God-passion always kills the thing it loves."[1]

But the prophetic thunder is oddly momentary and capricious. Sometimes it thunders on one side, sometimes on the other ; we must go back, we must go forward ; sometimes sex is the way to life, sometimes chastity is " infinitely dear ". It does not take us long to see that the prophecies are often a *cri du cœur*, that the prophet is often speaking, not for all men, but for himself. Most artists do the same. But with the great artist we commonly find that personal emotions have been universalized ; we are enabled to appropriate them as our own. Lawrence's emotional experience, as we have seen, is such as only by a miracle could become comprehensible to the normal man. It begins

[1] " Kangaroo ", p. 222 (Secker).

46

with two disastrous sexual encounters ; it continues
with a reaction away from the " spiritual " woman and
towards the physical woman which is in its way as
perilous. The verse is almost silent on the subject of
his war experiences, but from the prose we learn that
he was suspected of spying and actually ordered to
leave the county of Cornwall ; his treatment by the
military authorities engendered in him a bitterness and
shame which far exceeded ordinary suffering. Henceforth he nurses an animosity against society which
influences all his teaching, which makes him shrink yet
more painfully from unsympathetic contact, which
urges him to yet more frenzied contempt and loathing
for the common herd. This must be borne in mind
in any attempt to reconcile the contradictions of his
creed. His attack on society, just as much as his attack
on the modern use of sex, is rooted in the personal.

But often genius works the miracle, and Lawrence's
fantastic, undisciplined emotions are universalized ;
they grow common to us all. And once we accept
them it is impossible to hold him a failure as a person.
He spent his life in friction ; he saw, as he thought,
the way to " blessedness " only to lose sight of it in
fruitless warfare. But let it not be forgotten that he
once saw a way and had the courage to point others
to it. Whatever degree of failure may be imputed to
him is largely the result, not of a fault, but of a virtue
in excess. Sensitiveness made his participation in life
a matter of acute suffering ; it turned every misfortune
into a catastrophe. He came to feel himself marked

down for catastrophe ; his agonies were superhuman. In the end, of course, he began to rend his own flesh, to outrage his own sensibilities ; his very delicacy turned to sadism. Yet this sensitiveness it was which gave him the clue to many hidden things. He understood, not with his mind, but with his feelings ; he would be subtly *aware* of an idea, a book, a human being. In the letters we read how, looking at a Cornish valley with its gorse and blackthorn, he felt that " the sense of something, someone magnificent approaching, is so strong, it is a wonder one does not see visions in the heavens ".[1] Such sensibilities were always there ; but they reacted most strongly to physical stimuli ; where the stimuli were mental or spiritual he translated them into terms of the physical. The truth is that the sensitiveness itself had its origins in the physical ; it was a sensitiveness proceeding from " touch ". And so we come back ; what was the essence of the writer was a danger to the man ; sensibility made him a poet but nearly wrecked his life.

I have tried to show in some detail how this physical quality rules his work ; how the sensuous colours and images, the shape and movement of his verse spring from an almost intolerable physical apprehension. To ignore this, as Mr. Murry does, and to substitute for the " touchstone of caresses " the figure of a " Christian ascetic " posing as an " oriental polygamist " [2] is to betray an insensibility to style unparalleled in criticism.

[1] " Letters ", p. 408 (Heinemann).
[2] " Son of Woman ", p. 279.

As Miss Jane Soames has pointed out,[1] Lawrence spent
his life struggling against the Puritanism in which he
had been bred ; he hated it, though he could never
wholly escape from it. He was a Puritan by upbringing, not by natural inclination. And here we are confronted with the dualism which split his writings as
well as his life. The Puritan is always at war with
the natural physical man. The reformer plagues the
creature of moods, the " meeting place for sun and
rain ", who longs to let things be. The light gods fight
against the dark gods in his being, the mind and spirit
against the urgent blood. But let us make no mistake ;
Lawrence does not, ultimately, deny the light gods. It
is their supremacy which he denies. For him modern
civilization is the logical conclusion of an error : the
error of Christianity, which rejected the body : the
error of woman, who puts away her natural birthright
in favour of an imagined spiritual ascendancy. The
balance must be redressed ; we must renew our allegiance to the dark gods : woman must learn once more
to submit and leave to man " the responsibility for the
next step into the future ". [2]

Within Lawrence himself, meanwhile, the balance
rocks and tilts ; the conflict rages on. He loves, he
hates ; he must have contact, he must be alone ; he
dominates, he shrinks ; he is inviolable, he is persecuted.
And yet at the centre there is something consistent ;

[1] " Life and Letters ", December, 1932.
[2] " Fantasia of the Unconscious " (Adelphi Library Edition),
p. 112 (Secker).

49

there is " the profound sensual experience of truth ".
In Mr. T. S. Eliot we have a Puritan who submits to
his Puritanism ; Lawrence never submits, and never
reconciles the opposing principles. He is never even
in search of harmony. After death, maybe, the harmony which is in oblivion.

> . . . in unknown Death we perhaps shall know
> Oneness and poised immunity.

But life is dependent on conflict ; man is

> a creature of conflict, like a cataract :

he is eternally opposed to himself :

> And while we live
> the kissing and communing cannot cease
> nor yet the striving and the horrid strife.

Eternal opposition—and eternal change. Life can
never be static ; it is for ever moving through death
to rebirth. Lawrence sees civilization dying round
him ; very well then, it must die, but it shall be reborn,
and so with each man and woman. It has never to
my knowledge been fully recognized that this is the
pivot of his work : the idea of renewal and resurrection.
In the poetry it becomes explicit only towards the end
of his life ; but from the letters we can see how early
it took hold of him. It is already present in the pro-
posed foreword to " Sons and Lovers " (January,
1913).[1] In the second year of the War he is preach-

[1] " Letters ", pp. 95–102.

ing the necessity for the spiritual rebirth of the individual and of society ; " there must be a new heaven
and a new earth, and a new heart and soul : all new :
a pure resurrection ".[1] He urges his friends to " dare
to go down, and be killed, to die in this self ".[2] He
himself must suffer the death in his relations with his
wife : " It is a fight one has to fight—the old Adam
to be killed in me, the old Eve in her—then a new
Adam and a new Eve ".[3] Whole nations must die
before the resurrection ; there must be " a vast death-
happening " [4] in America ; the Austrians " are *en route*
to their death ; and, let us hope, resurrection ".[5]
Ideas must be reborn ; leadership must be reborn ;
" we're only in the dying stage as yet ".[6] Sometimes
he feels that the way to the new heaven and the new
earth may be cleared by a revolution—" a real bust-
up, quite purposeless and aimless ".[7]

> Damned loutish bolshevists,
> Who perhaps will do the business after all,
> In the long run, in spite of themselves.

Sometimes he longs to outdistance the process of disintegration by founding a little colony, an Utopia—on
the slopes of the Andes, in Florida, on an island, anywhere out of the world. But the plan is never carried
out—perhaps because he knows that, wherever he is,
he must still pass through " the waters of oblivion ".
Mr. Murry says that Lawrence took the way of dis-

[1] Ibid., p. 279. [2] Ibid., p. 296. [3] Ibid., p. 372.
[4] Ibid., p. 565. [5] Ibid., p. 705. [6] Ibid., p. 704.
                   [7] Ibid., p. 406.

51

solution.[1] So he did—because he was convinced that only through dissolution could life be attained. And it is because sex affords us a minor oblivion, a minor dissolution, that it is so important.

> It is the major part of being, this having surpassed oneself, this having touched the edge of the beyond, and perished, yet not perished.

Sex is an epitome of the eternal process of death and regeneration. Through it man is reborn of woman; it is a foretaste of resurrection and a promise of eternal life. In " Last Poems " Lawrence is on the brink of a major consummation :

> The end of all knowledge is oblivion
> sweet, dark oblivion, when I cease
> even from myself, and am consummated.

But the cycle is always the same : the movement of the seasons through " the deep oblivion of earth's lapse and renewal " ; the oblivion and rebirth of sex ; the surrender and resurrection of the individual in life ; the surrender and resurrection of the individual in death. If we bear in mind this ruling passion for regeneration much that is obscure in Lawrence's work becomes clear. And most of all it clarifies his attitude towards sex— sex, a way to rebirth and a way to separate being. For in rebirth there is no confusion, no mingling ; none of the engulfing of the " isolated being " which he dreaded in " love ".

. . . .

[1] " Son of Woman ", p. 134.

The doctrine of regeneration is not novel nor, in Lawrence's work, is it complete, since we are never told how we are to achieve the renunciation of our old selves. And for the rest his creed is not a creed for universal acceptance. The ordinary man is indifferent to the idea of separate being and untouched by the psychological problems which convulsed Lawrence's life. For all his resistance to " the white mind " Lawrence is compelled to use intellectual persuasion ; and it is usually a persuasion beyond the grasp of the casual reader. Since, then, he is neither an originator nor an easy teacher, to what can we ascribe his popular success ? Partly, I think, to misunderstanding. His truculence, his fanatical outspokenness, his output of " phallic " [1] novels and poems and pictures attracted more readers than his genius ever won ; the public mistook the moralist for the pornographer. His incoherent reasoning, his undisciplined emotionalism hoodwinked the semi-intellectuals whom he despised ; his contempt for tradition was hailed as a call to a freedom his inexorable conscience would have abhorred. Sometimes, it is true, his views are those advanced by the cheap Press ; sometimes he pauses to inveigh against

flat-chested, crop-headed, chemicalized women, of indeterminate sex,

and wimbly-wambly young men, of sex still more indeterminate.

When we find Lawrence adding his authority to such banality we can better understand his popular reputa-

[1] " Letters ", p. 710.

tion. But there is in his work a basis for a great and lasting reputation. However illogical his arguments, however distorted by personal animus his views, he stands, finally, on the right side ; he stands for individuality against mechanization, for the complete man against the incomplete man, for life against death. A moral rather than an intellectual force, he lends to a familiar solution of the problem the power of a terrific emotional intensity. And when all is said and done he is a great writer. A great writer careless of perfection, capable of shoddiness and even grossness of style ; but still, by virtue of his vitality, his shattering command of language and the rare sharpness of his sensibilities, a great writer. Out of the torment of his being is born, like ambergris, a violent sensuous poetry. His life declines to its winter ; but from the brink of dissolution it still puts forth blossoms and perfume.

and still, among it all, snatches of lovely oblivion, and snatches
    of renewal
odd, wintry flowers upon the withered stem, yet new, strange
    flowers
such as my life has not brought forth before, new blossoms
    of me—

then I must know that still
I am in the hands of the unknown God,
he is breaking me down to his own oblivion
to send me forth on a new morning, a new man.

Oblivion and renewal, death and rebirth—Lawrence's message is clear enough. For it is indeed the resurrection of the body and the life everlasting.

54

T. S. ELIOT

T. S. ELIOT

" I am used ", Mr. T. S. Eliot once wrote, "to having cosmic significances, which I never suspected, extracted from my work (such as it is) by enthusiastic persons at a distance ; and to being informed that something which I meant seriously is *vers de société* ; and to having my personal biography reconstructed from passages which I had got out of books, or which I invented out of nothing because they sounded well ; and to having my biography invariably ignored in what I *did* write from personal experience." [1] It would be only natural to remark that Mr. Eliot has himself to blame if he is misconstrued, since he has put so many traps in the way of the enthusiastic person at a distance. The complaint, however, is interesting since it implies that, contrary to the belief of the opponents of " modernist " poetry, Mr. Eliot means to be understood. I shall do my best in this essay not to neglect such indications of meaning and explanations of form as he has himself supplied.

[1] " Shakespeare and the Stoicism of Seneca " (1927 : Oxford University Press).

57

Let us look at the extent of the material with which we have to deal.

In 1917 [1] there appeared a volume of twelve poems with the title " Prufrock "—a volume remarkable for the audacity of its images, for the violence of its contrasts, for its obscurity, and for the disgust with which it viewed a frowsy world. Two years later it was followed by " Poems " (six new pieces), and in 1920 by " Ara Vus Prec ", which added seven new poems to the existing material ; the obscurity deepened, and any friend to the vernal gaieties of Georgian verse might have been excused for supposing that this was the Antichrist in English poetry, the Rebel against authority, had not Mr. Eliot in the latter year explained his " programme for the *métier* of poetry " and avowed his respect for tradition in a book of critical essays, " The Sacred Wood ". The year 1923 produced a long poem of protean form, " The Waste Land ", and a measure of assistance ; for Mr. Eliot, taking pity on his readers, appended to this vision of decay several pages of explanatory notes. In 1925 " Poems, 1909–1925 " was published ; it included " Prufrock " ; the 1919 " Poems " and six pieces from " Ara Vus Prec " (henceforth referred to collectively as the 1920 " Poems ") ; " The Waste Land " ; and a poem of four pages, " The Hollow Men ". From that date to the beginning of 1930 Mr. Eliot published no collection of poetry and only a very few single pieces. Of these, " Fragment

[1] Dates given are, where possible, those of publication in book form in England.

of a Prologue " (1926) and "Fragment of an Agon "
(1927),[1] two of the brothel scenes in which Mr. Eliot
excels, echoed the despair of "The Hollow Men ";
but in "Journey of the Magi " (1927), "A Song for
Simeon " (1928) and "Animula " (1929) admirers of
the earlier verse were surprised to discover a steadily
strengthening religious feeling. It would have been
hardly possible, however, to base upon this material
an estimate of a new orientation had not Mr. Eliot,
between 1925 and 1930, produced as well a small body
of prose. There were many indications here that the
writer was approaching the Christian point of view ;
but the output was not large and the indications were
not definite, and it was a relief when, at the end of
1928, he published a second book of critical essays,
"For Lancelot Andrewes ", with a preface declaring
roundly that his " general point of view " was " classicist
in literature, royalist in politics, and anglo-catholic in
religion ".[2] Mr. Eliot seemed to have changed his
mind with a vengeance since the 1925 " Poems " with
their unorthodox forms and their emphasis on dissolution. The year 1930 produced " Ash Wednesday ", a

[1] Both these dramatic fragments originally appeared in the
" Criterion ", but have now been published in book form under the
title " Sweeney Agonistes " (1932 : Faber & Faber).
[2] Cf. " After Strange Gods ", p. 27 : " The facility with which
this statement has been quoted has helped to reveal to me that as
it stands the statement is injudicious. . . . I now see the danger
of suggesting to outsiders that the Faith is a political principle or
a literary fashion, and the sum of all a dramatic posture " (1934 :
Faber & Faber).

sequence of six religious poems which, by their revelation of spiritual endeavour, consolidated the evidence which had gone before, and " Marina ", a single poem which marked the arrival at a stage where that endeavour had been for the first time rewarded. Since " Marina " two poems, " Triumphal March " (1931) and " Difficulties of a Statesman " (1932), seem to abandon the religious mood ; in reality they have merely extended the search for inward peace. " Five-Finger Exercises " (" Criterion ", January, 1933), a group of five brilliant exercises in plagiarism and parody ; and two purely lyrical pieces, " Words for Music " (" Virginia Quarterly Review ", April, 1934), constituted a two years' poetic output of average dimensions ; it was not till the summer of 1934 that the material was substantially increased by the publication of " The Rock ", a " pageant play " including between eight and nine hundred verse lines. The play was designed for public performance ; it was written under ecclesiastical auspices and submissive to " expert " supervision. For its prose dialogue we need not blame Mr. Eliot ; the choruses and other verse passages, conditioned though they are by the circumstances of their composition, must be considered in any estimate of his work.

From here the reader, looking back, can trace a development up to a point of view which does not seem likely to be radically altered. He can survey the several parts with which he must reckon in forming a judgment of Mr. Eliot : the " modernist " poet ; the critic whose theories explain the eccentricities of the poet ; the Christian whose belief has lately permeated the criticism and supplied the emotional basis of the poetry ; all joining in the editor of a serious literary quarterly, " The Criterion ". And, marking the modest extent, up till now, of the material in poetry—one poem of 433 lines, a dramatic fragment, the choruses of a pageant and about four dozen short poems (if we leave out Mr. Eliot's translation of S.-J. Perse's " Anabase ")—he will feel it essential to miss nothing. All very well for Mr. Eliot to complain of being over-explained. A Victor Hugo with his enormous output can afford to spend words on nothing ; it is natural to suppose that Mr. Eliot *meant* every syllable.

Let us look to see what meaning we can find in the poems. Let us also admit frankly that it will not always be easy to find any meaning at all.[1] But at least it should be possible to discover a mood, a general direction of thought ; to follow the development of that mood from its early to its later stages ; to see, in fact, what attitude Mr. Eliot adopts in face of the Waste Land of society and civilization.

The first poem in the 1925 volume, " The Love Song of J. Alfred Prufrock ", opens with a discord. The evening is

> . . . spread out against the sky
> Like a patient etherized upon a table ;

---

[1] Easier, however, than Mr. John Sparrow implies in his interesting " Sense and Poetry " (Constable).

What a shock for ears accustomed to the smooth
sequences of the neo-Wordsworthians ! The discord,
it is true, had been used often enough by the Georgians :
by Masefield, by Rupert Brooke ; but there it was too
often a mannerism ; here it is the basis of the poem.
Prufrock, as Mr. Bonamy Dobrée has pointed out,[1] is
a middle-aged man boggling at the idea of an affair,
unable to rid himself of a suspicion that success may
prove disappointing, acutely conscious of cutting an
incongruous figure in a drawing-room.

> And indeed there will be time
> To wonder, " Do I dare ? " and, " Do I dare ? "
> Time to turn back and descend the stair,
> With a bald spot in the middle of my hair—
> (They will say : " How his hair is growing thin ! ")

The poem is, in fact, concerned with fitting together
incongruities. Prufrock cannot reconcile his own character with the romantic situation into which he foresees
himself drawn ; he cannot reconcile either with the
anti-social passions of which he is momentarily aware.

> I should have been a pair of ragged claws
> Scuttling across the floors of silent seas.

Of these clashing elements none can be victorious ; an
air of defeat hangs about even the descriptive passages
of the poem :

> . . . certain half-deserted streets,
> The muttering retreats
> Of restless nights in one-night cheap hotels
> And sawdust restaurants with oyster-shells :

---

[1] " The Lamp and the Lute ", p. 111 (Clarendon Press).

And the emotional discord is echoed in the contrast between satirical and imaginative expression :

Shall I part my hair behind ?   Do I dare to eat a peach ?
I shall wear white flannel trousers, and walk upon the beach.
I have heard the mermaids singing, each to each.

I do not think that they will sing to me.

I have seen them riding seaward on the waves
Combing the white hair of the waves blown back
When the wind blows the water white and black.

We have lingered in the chambers of the sea
By sea-girls wreathed with seaweed red and brown
Till human voices wake us, and we drown.

The second poem, " Portrait of a Lady ", reverses the situation ; here it is the woman who makes tentative advances to a man younger than herself. The use of contrast is still evident, though less evident than in " Prufrock " ; more remarkable is the general feeling of regret and irresolution. Again the man has been vanquished by something in his circumstances and in himself, prevented from taking a decisive step,

Doubtful, for a while
Not knowing what to feel or if I understand
Or whether wise or foolish, tardy or too soon. . . .

This melancholy alternates with the disgust which modern society arouses in Mr. Eliot. We meet it several times in the " Prufrock " volume, at its best in " La Figlia Che Piange ", a picture of the parting of two lovers, because there most adequately related to its source.

> She turned away, but with the autumn weather
> Compelled my imagination many days,
> Many days and many hours :
> Her hair over her arms and her arms full of flowers.
> And I wonder how they should have been together !
> I should have lost a gesture and a pose.
> Sometimes these cogitations still amaze
> The troubled midnight and the noon's repose.

I quote this poem less for its mood than for its manner ; Mr. Eliot, with his soft-foot repetitions and his subtle vowel-sequence, can write a conventionally " poetic " passage as well as anyone. In violent contrast are his sketches of suburban life, " Preludes " and " Morning at the Window ". Here Mr. Eliot piles up murky and squalid images to make a picture of a decaying genteel society (in which the housemaid is high priestess) :

> They are rattling breakfast plates in basement kitchens,
> And along the trampled edges of the street
> I am aware of the damp souls of housemaids
> Sprouting despondently at area gates.

It is a world in which morning means only the resumption of a dingy masquerade, and evening brings nothing better than

> The burnt-out ends of smoky days.

Nor does Mr. Eliot find relief in contemplating the higher strata of middle-class society. Discord and

defeat, squalor and stupidity—a mind aware of such
a state of things must at times feel existence intolerable ;
and in one poem hideous images and the agonies of
recollection force a crisis :

> The lamp said,
> " Four o'clock,
> Here is the number on the door.
> Memory !
> You have the key,
> The little lamp spreads a ring on the stair,
> Mount.
> The bed is open ; the tooth-brush hangs on the wall,
> Put your shoes at the door, sleep, prepare for life."
>
> The last twist of the knife.

There is no great difficulty, then, in the first volume
of poems in seeing with what kind of an intelligence
we have to deal. It is an intelligence which, since it
desires harmony, order and seemliness, cannot but
expose whenever it finds them discord, confusion and
squalor. It is an intelligence capable of subtle and even
profound perceptions, but contenting itself, except on
one or two occasions, with the observation of externals.
The result of the observation is often harshly expressed
because the externals are harsh, and because Mr. Eliot
believes in twisting the knife himself when he can ; one
of his talents at this stage is that of choosing the most
grating descriptive weapon. And it is obscurely
expressed because he uses to sharpen his contrasts
material which apparently he does not trouble to
correlate.

Contenting itself, I have said, with the observation of externals. I do not mean to deny that Mr. Eliot's back-street scenes imply discontent with the fabric of society. I do not mean to deny that his Conversation Pieces imply an acquaintance with the disquiet of the heart. But as yet he is mainly occupied with looking at people and things and with *feeling* ; he has not organized his impressions and emotions into a *criticism* of society. In the 1920 " Poems " we see the beginning of such an organization. At a first glance we see something quite different. The discovery in " Prufrock " of an undisguised piece of prose left the reader puzzled but respectful. He is even less certain of his ground when in the 1920 collection he finds several poems in French (one, for instance, a parody of Tristan Corbière) [1] ; when he finds the English poems dotted with strange names—Mr. Silvero, Hakagawa, Madame de Tornquist, Fräulein von Kulp, De Bailhache, Fresca, Mrs. Cammel, Burbank, Bleistein, Princess Volupine, Sweeney—which, whether or not they can be traced in history or fiction, evade the acquaintance of the average person. (Somebody ought to compile a dictionary of Eliot mythology.) Nor is the reader's confidence restored when he discovers certain of these characters to be inventions ; when he sees, for instance, that Princess Volupine is a Venetian Lesbia, and Sweeney a plain-clothes Caliban. But with the creation of these types Mr. Eliot begins to concentrate his quarrels with society. He no longer simply expresses

[1] " Mélange adultère de tout."

disgust with the present ; he begins to compare it with
the past. More and more he uses contrast, but
he handles it less crudely than in the earlier poems,
bringing the elements into a more easily recognized
relation.

> The host with someone indistinct
> Converses at the door apart,
> The nightingales are singing near
> The Convent of the Sacred Heart,
>
> And sang within the bloody wood
> When Agamemnon cried aloud,
> And let their liquid siftings fall
> To stain the stiff dishonoured shroud.

Thus, in one of the Sweeney poems, by the contrast of
ugly and beautiful, and the relation of past and present,
a description of a rowdy dinner with women of easy
virtue is translated into an indictment.

The decay which Mr. Eliot in his earlier book observed
to be attacking society he now sees going deeper than
he at first showed. Mr. Robert Graves and Miss Laura
Riding [1] have ingeniously explained the poem " Burbank with a Baedeker : Bleistein with a Cigar " as
dealing with the decline of Venice under the usurping
Jew.

> The smoky candle-end of time
>
> Declines. On the Rialto once.
> The rats are underneath the piles.
> The jew is underneath the lot.

---

[1] " A Survey of Modernist Poetry ", p. 236 (Heinemann).

It has been pointed out that the rats are responsible for a great deal in Mr. Eliot's despairing visions. More important than a first encounter with a recurrent symbol is the allusiveness of the poem. In the space of a rhyming four-line stanza we find references to Shakespeare ; adapted quotations ; quotations frankly filched. I shall discuss this method presently. The maiden city, meanwhile, is seduced, culture violated ; and Philosophy's charms are withered. Mr. Eliot remembers how Webster stirred the senses by dwelling on the paraphernalia of death, how Donne, too,

> . . . knew the anguish of the marrow
> The ague of the skeleton ;

The senses still bestow their consolations :

> Grishkin is nice ; her Russian eye
> Is underlined for emphasis ;
> Uncorseted, her friendly bust
> Gives promise of pneumatic bliss.

But thought, grown dessicated, has lost all relation to the sensual life :

> . . . our lot crawls between dry ribs
> To keep our metaphysic warm.

There is no flesh on the bones of philosophy to-day. Poetry, too, has fallen into disrepute :

> Misunderstood
> The accents of the now retired
> Profession of the calamus.

68

Finally, Mr. Eliot satirizes the decay of religion **and** the Church :

> At mating time the hippo's voice
> Betrays inflexions hoarse and odd,
> But every week we hear rejoice
> The Church, at being one with God.
>
> The hippopotamus's day
> Is passed in sleep ; at night he hunts ;
> God works in a mysterious way—
> The Church can sleep and feed at once.
>
> I saw the 'potamus take wing
> Ascending from the damp savannas,
> And quiring angels round him sing
> The praise of God, in loud hosannas.
>
> Blood of the Lamb shall wash him clean
> And him shall heavenly arms enfold,
> Among the saints he shall be seen
> Performing on a harp of gold.
>
> He shall be washed as white as snow,
> By all the martyr'd virgins kist,
> While the True Church remains below
> Wrapt in the old miasmal mist.

The satire is directed, not against faith, but against its decay into formula ; the very violence of the attack on a sham implies feeling for the reality. But the sham triumphs, the reality fades ; only disillusion persists.

> But where is the penny world I bought
>   To eat with Pipit behind the screen ?
> The red-eyed scavengers are creeping
>   From Kentish Town and Golder's Green ;

Where are the eagles and the trumpets?

Buried beneath some snow-deep Alps.
Over buttered scones and crumpets
Weeping, weeping multitudes
Droop in a hundred A.B.C.'s.

Society is mouldering away together with its intellectual and religious basis ; it remains for Mr. Eliot to give a panoramic impression of the moment before the crash. " The Waste Land " supplies that impression.

" Not only the title ", writes Mr. Eliot, " but the plan and a good deal of the incidental symbolism of the poem were suggested by Miss Jessie L. Weston's book on the Grail legend : *From Ritual to Romance*." His critics have gratefully taken the tip. It will not, therefore, be necessary for me to recapitulate Miss Weston's arguments for the sexual significance of the Grail legend and its origin in fertility rites, or to repeat the story of the land wasted and waterless because of the sickness of the Fisher King, the spell which could be broken only when Percival reached the Chapel Perilous, the Chapel of the Grail. Equipped with Miss Weston's book and with Mr. Eliot's own notes (for the modern poet does not always abandon his work to the Theobalds of a future age), the reader may gather a general idea of its purport.[1] To understand it in detail Mr.

---

[1] Since this essay was written detailed analyses of " The Waste Land " have been supplied by Mr. F. R. Leavis, in " New Bearings in English Poetry ", a serious study of the present state of poetry (Chatto & Windus), and by Mr. Hugh Ross Williamson in " The Poetry of T. S. Eliot " (Hodder & Stoughton).

Eliot implies that he would require an acquaintance with " The Golden Bough ", Dante, the Elizabethan dramatists, Baudelaire and the French symbolists, St. Augustine, the Buddha's Fire Sermon, the Upanishads, Ovid, Catullus, Sappho, Andrew Marvell, F. H. Bradley, Wagner's librettos and the fauna of North America. It is, in fact, a poem suited only to an Admirable Crichton. Less lettered, we may still find in it a synthesis of Mr. Eliot's perceptions of decay ; many have accepted it as expressing " the plight of a whole generation ". The allusive style has been carried here to its limits. Public-house talk jostles phrases from Webster and Shakespeare. Tiresias is made witness of the seduction of a typist whose " folly " elicits a revised version of the Goldsmith lyric " When lovely woman ". A popular song is sandwiched between an adapted quotation from Marvell and a parody of some lines in Day's " Parliament of Bees " and a scrap of Verlaine. Each fragment Mr. Eliot has built into his structure evokes, naturally, its own associated ideas. In juxtaposition it evokes many more, so that the *suggestions* of the poem as a whole are almost endless. And the abrupt transitions from one set of emotions to another (for Mr. Eliot, whatever he may say about fusion, is sometimes intentionally disjointed) combine with the varied metres to give an impression of instability appropriate to the main theme, the decadence of Europe and the despair of the individual. Despair comes in many shapes. There is the realization of death, " fear in a handful of dust ". There is the realization of aimlessness :

71

" What shall I do now ? What shall I do ?
I shall rush out as I am, and walk the street
With my hair down, so. What shall we do to-morrow ?
What shall we ever do ? "

> The hot water at ten.
> And if it rains, a closed car at four.
> And we shall play a game of chess,
> Pressing lidless eyes and waiting for a knock upon the door.

Intimations of mortality ; the tedium of wealth and
the sordidness of poverty ; to these Mr. Eliot adds such
a picture of mean and stupid vice as one does not forget.
By an astonishing feat of co-ordination he makes the
seduction of the typist the crisis of a section in which
the theme of the flowing Thames binds together
Ferdinand of " The Tempest ", an amorous Smyrna
merchant, Leicester in Elizabeth's barge and the three
Thames maidens, fallen sisters of the Rhine maidens ;
while Tiresias, in whom both sexes, seducer and seduced,
meet, " foresuffers " all. The final degradation has
been reached ; the abyss opens ; and the last section
of the poem shows us the crash.

> Here is no water but only rock
> Rock and no water and the sandy road
> The road winding above among the mountains
> Which are mountains of rock without water
> If there were water we should stop and drink
> Amongst the rock one cannot stop or think
> Sweat is dry and feet are in the sand
> If there were only water amongst the rock
> Dead mountain mouth of carious teeth that cannot spit
> Here one can neither stand nor lie nor sit

There is not even silence in the mountains
But dry sterile thunder without rain
There is not even solitude in the mountains
But red sullen faces sneer and snarl
From doors of mudcracked houses

Then the storm breaks with a final great clap of thunder :

London Bridge is falling down falling down falling down
Poi s'ascose nel foco che gli affina
Quando fiam ceu chelidon—O swallow swallow
Le Prince d'Aquitaine à la tour abolie
These fragments I have shored against my ruins
Why then Ile fit you. Hieronymo's mad againe.
Datta. Dayadhvam. Damyata.
    Shantih shantih shantih

Dante, Catullus, Gerard de Nerval, Kyd, the Upanishads —everything topples about our ears. The last Judgment is come.

We have traced the development of Mr. Eliot's mood of despair from its early expression to its culmination in " The Waste Land ". We have seen him at first discomfited by life, sensitive to discord and squalor, even tortured by them. Next we have found him concentrating on one or two aspects of civilization, making definite attacks, satirizing a decadent Church, an empty system of thought, a degraded morality. Finally, we have seen him sum up the desperate situation of a Europe facing life and death without the spiritual and intellectual certainties which sustained an earlier generation. Yet even from the despair of " The Waste

Land " there emerges some kind of a solution to Mr. Eliot's problems.

> The awful daring of a moment's surrender
> Which an age of prudence can never retract
> By this, and this only, we have existed

For a moment, in accepting the challenge implied in his own picture of a world in collapse, Mr. Eliot ventures an affirmation ; something stable seems to be rising from the ruins, order has been created from chaos. But I do not think it is a solution which could ever have satisfied him for long. Mr. Eliot was looking for an order which he had not himself invented ; he was looking for Authority. He had not yet found it ; the knife was to give one more twist. In " The Hollow Men " (1925) decay had reached the stage of disintegration.

> This is the dead land
> This is the cactus land
> Here the stone images
> Are raised, here they receive
> The supplication of a dead man's hand
> Under the twinkle of a fading star.

And in " Sweeney Agonistes " (1926–7) death knocks at the door of the brothel itself. These two " fragments of an Aristophanic melodrama " are written in staccato dialogue which repeats itself in mechanical rhythms and breaks now and again into a syncopated chorus. Mr. Eliot uses the form of musical drama, and the resources of jazz and the Gilbertian jingle, to indicate the inexorable cycle of " birth, and copulation, and death ". It is the union of the ultimate economy of diction with a conception of the ultimate spiritual destitution. Aridity can be no further denuded. When his next poem appeared it was the poem of a man who had found a path out of " cactus land ".

At the end of 1927 there was published a single poem, " Journey of the Magi ". The first lines are adapted from a prose passage of Lancelot Andrewes ; but the mood of the poem is very different from the mood of a seventeenth-century divine. To the Wise Man who describes his journey the revelation of the Birth brings only disquiet. He is left

. . . no longer at ease here, in the old dispensation,

renunciation of a past is the first step to the acceptance of a new order, and the interim is doubt and pain. It is the initial stage of the Christian life. When, a year later, a second single poem, " A Song for Simeon ", was published the poet was on the same path. Into the mouth of Simeon is put a second *Nunc Dimittis* ; but in his prayer for release we hear the voice of the believer who shrinks from the stony ground.

I am tired with my own life and the lives of those after me, I am dying in my own death and the deaths of those after me.

It is Tiresias of " The Waste Land " over again, but a Tiresias acquainted with salvation. And that he has not yet left the desert behind him is shown in a third poem, " Animula " (1929), which describes the wanderings of a soul no less defenceless than Hadrian's and concludes with a prayer for all sojourners on earth.

75

Mr. Eliot has, in fact, not changed his opinion about the confusion and sordidness of life. He has found an answer to its problems ; but there is no cleavage between the mood of " The Waste Land " and that of the poems immediately following it. The continuity is still clearer when we come to " Ash Wednesday ". Here for the first time in the poetry is an unmistakable statement of Mr. Eliot's solution. The uncertainty of the first stage in the Christian progress is past ; now the believer spends himself in the struggle towards the divine. He renounces the " infirm glory of the positive hour ", no longer desiring, in Shakespearean phrase, " this man's gift and that man's scope " ; he submits to the knowledge of death and welcomes its peace ; he puts aside the distractions of the world

> Fading, fading ; strength beyond hope and despair
> Climbing the third stair.

But still after regeneration the vision withdraws and the soul is shut out from its divine home ; still after the revelation of the Word self-will and the flesh have to be reckoned with.

> And the lost heart stiffens and rejoices
> In the lost lilac and the lost sea voices
> And the weak spirit quickens to rebel
> For the bent golden-rod and the lost sea smell
> Quickens to recover
> The cry of quail and the whirling plover
> And the blind eye creates
> The empty forms between the ivory gates
> And smell renews the salt savour of the sandy earth

There must be intercession for those who

> . . . are terrified and cannot surrender
> And affirm before the world and deny between the rocks
> In the last desert between the last blue rocks
> The desert in the garden the garden in the desert
> Of drouth, spitting from the mouth the withered apple-seed.

And the sequence ends with a prayer for submission :

> Teach us to sit still
> Even among these rocks,

Even now the rock is waterless and the way lies through waste ground. Only once does the traveller come in sight of his promised land—in " Marina ". Then, indeed, the material world and its snares become insubstantial in face of an ineffable reality :

This form, this face, this life
Living to live in a world of time beyond me ; let me
Resign my life for this life, my speech for that unspoken,
The awakened, lips parted, the hope, the new ships.

In an ecstasy the soul recognizes the heavenly country towards which it has been striving ; and the stony ground is forgotten at the first promise of a divine peace. But confusion returns, serenity falters ; once more the spirit sojourns in the desert. " Triumphal March " and " Difficulties of a Statesman " represent the endeavour to achieve, not isolation, but indifference in the midst of confusion : the longing of the soul exhausted by conflict and complexity to retreat within itself, to be hidden

> At the still point of the turning world.

In "The Rock" Mr. Eliot is compelled by the
exigencies of his medium to submerge the personal.
The pageant was written for performance on behalf of
the Forty-Five Churches Fund of the Diocese of London ; as I have implied, he was not a free agent in
its composition. Cactus land is not a theme welcomed
on the public stage, or calculated to enrich a benevolent
organization ; and we must not be hasty to ascribe
the diminution of aridity to a new geniality on the part
of the author. The play is concerned with the building of a church by modern workmen ; but repeatedly
it harks back to the building of other churches—Sabert's
church, St. Bartholomew's, Edward the Confessor's
Westminster, St. Paul's. The verse is used sometimes
for the purpose of narrative, sometimes as a commentary
on the action ; it ranges from a music-hall song, through
a satirical scene attacking the new creeds of communism
and fascism and the old creed of capitalism, to passages
reminiscent in mood and manner of the psalms. The
first chorus is an indictment of a society endowed with

Knowledge of words, and ignorance of the Word.

—the second of a community " born to idleness, to
frittered lives and squalid deaths, embittered scorn in
honeyless hives " ; England itself is a waste land in-
habited by those blameless hollow men the unemployed.
There are frequent echoes of the earlier work. Men
huddle in

Subsiding basements where the rat breeds

78

—the city will decay to " a street of scattered brick where the goat climbs " ; the Rock, like Tiresias, has " foresuffered " all :

I have known two worlds, I have known two worlds of death.
All that you suffer, I have suffered before,
And suffer always, even to the end of the world.

Always the desert lies in wait, the desert whence comes the Stranger Death.[1] And there are touches of the austerity which informs " Ash Wednesday " and makes of Mr. Eliot's Christianity such " bitter consolation ". But the agonized resignation of " Ash Wednesday ", the exhaustion of " Difficulties of a Statesman ", are mitigated here. The style is direct, and less packed than in any poem since " A Song for Simeon " (except " Words for Music "). The allusions are such as should be comprehensible to an audience familiar with the Bible and the Book of Common Prayer. Contrast, where it occurs, is simple, even elementary, but used without the jarring impact of the " Prufrock " poems. There is little here to alarm the timid reader ; almost one begins to question Mr. Eliot's right to be called difficult. " The Rock ", one sees, is partly a lending of his talent and reputation ; for this reason we cannot, without further evidence, base upon it an estimate of a new technical development. But it is also an opportunity for his talent. In the choruses he has bent to

[1] The Stranger is sometimes Death, sometimes the Rock (" The Witness. The Critic. The Stranger "). Cf. the symbolism of Mr. Auden's poem " The Witnesses " (see p. 181).

his own ends a theme imposed on him ; and he has made of the play a challenge, the challenge of light to the powers of darkness which he sees hemming in the race of men.[1]

Mr. Eliot's Christianity is a logical move from the position of the earlier poems. It is easy enough to say that from disillusion to unquestioning belief is only a step, or that a drowning man must needs catch at the likeliest straw. But Mr. Eliot's very onslaught on an effete Christianity, as I have already said, implies a regard for the ages of faith. We have seen him in the 1925 " Poems " express increasing disgust with an unbelieving civilization. But he never wished to be counted with the unbelieving. " Doubt and uncertainty ", he writes, " are merely a variety of belief " [2] ; and in the doubt and uncertainty of " The Waste Land " are already the germs of belief. There is no cause for surprise in the Christianity of the later poems. A mind naturally prone to concern with problems of belief has found its creed ; a mind naturally repelled by disorder has accepted the order of the Church. Mr. Eliot has found the Authority without which his position in a world of shams had become intolerable.

Let us look to see what part, if any, authority plays in his poetic theory.

In trying to find a sequence of thought in the poetry we have noticed various peculiarities of method. I have drawn attention, for instance, to Mr. Eliot's use

---

[1] Cf. " After Strange Gods ", and see p. 169.
[2] " The Enemy ", January, 1927.

of contrast and implied comparison. His obscurity
needs no emphasis ; nor will anyone require to be told
that his imagery is daring and disquieting. The allusiveness and the learning which makes it possible are as
obvious. We have noticed that the methods are effective ; that contrast and implied comparison will serve
to drive home a point which without them might only
have pricked the skin ; that disquieting imagery is an
apt translation of disquieting ideas ; that allusion will
often suggest more to the reader than statement, and
that a little learning is a useful thing. But is there no
other explanation of a style sometimes so composed of
contrasts and quotations as to be almost unintelligible ?
Mr. Eliot has given the answer in his prose criticism,
notably in " The Sacred Wood ", a book which attempts
to do in a minor way for the present generation what
the " Deffense et Illustration " did for the France of
the Pléïade.

The idea of fusion, of course, underlies much of the
surface oddity. The ordinary person need not trouble
to correlate a taste for Spinoza with the noise of the
typewriter.[1] But in the mind of the poet, says Mr.
Eliot, disparate experiences are always forming new
wholes ; and in an essay often quoted he gives as
analogy the case of the catalytic agent which, remaining
itself unchanged, converts two separate substances into
a single substance.[2] " The poet's mind is in fact a

[1] Cf. " Homage to John Dryden ", p. 30 (Hogarth Press).
[2] But cf. " After Strange Gods ", p. 15 : " Some years ago I wrote
an essay entitled *Tradition and the Individual Talent.* During the course

receptacle for seizing and storing up numberless feelings, phrases, images, which remain there until all
the particles which can unite to form a new compound
are present together." [1] When the moment comes the
result is " a concentration, and a new thing resulting
from the concentration, of a very great number of
experiences which to the practical and active person
would not seem to be experiences at all ; it is a concentration which does not happen consciously or of
deliberation ".[2] One variety of this concentration Mr.
Eliot declares to be extinct : a variety which he calls
wit. Wit, in Mr. Eliot's sense, may imply an " alliance
of levity and seriousness (by which the seriousness is
intensified) " [3] such as we find in Marvell. It certainly
implies an equilibrium between dissimilar elements.
An alliance of levity and seriousness !—here is the
explanation of the satirical manner of " The Hippo-
potamus " and the changes of tone in the Sweeney
poems, here the excuse for the juxtaposition of Donne
and Grishkin, eagles and A.B.C.s. The modern reader,
accustomed to the smooth cadences of the Romantic
poets, is inclined to feel uncomfortable when he meets
such an alliance ; I do not think Mr. Eliot has always
been above forcing a jolt to shake the passenger. Every

of the subsequent fifteen years I have discovered, or had brought to
my attention, some unsatisfactory phrasing and at least one more than
doubtful analogy. But I do not repudiate what I wrote in that
essay any more fully than I should expect to do after such a lapse
of time."

[1] " The Sacred Wood ", p. 55 (second edition : Methuen).
[2] Ibid., p. 58.   [3] " Homage to John Dryden ", p. 38.

poet unconsciously concentrates his experiences. But Mr. Eliot, encouraged by his own theory, makes a point of concentrating ideas and images and phrases even less apparently related than Spinoza and the typewriter. The more disparate the " experiences " fused, the greater the imaginative effort the reader must make in order to grasp the new whole ; and should the fusion be incomplete, should " apeneck Sweeney " and Agamemnon, Grishkin and the Abstract Entities evade their new relationship, the poem must fall into unintelligible fragments. Mr. Eliot's genius for this poetic concentration is nearly always triumphant ; only rarely does the catalyst of his mind leave the elements still refractory. We must remember, however, that certain substances refuse to mix, and that Mr. Eliot's theory of concentration must be expected to work with difficulty where the materials are inherently incompatible. His poetic theory is, indeed, sometimes at loggerheads with his satirical purpose, with his desire to expose social discord and a fall from grace. To these mutinous subjects, as I hinted before, we must ascribe the harshness of many of the poems. " The only way of expressing emotion in the form of art is by finding an ' objective correlative ' ; in other words, a set of objects, a situation, a chain of events which shall be the formula of that *particular* emotion ; such that when the external facts, which must terminate in sensory experiences, are given, the emotion is immediately evoked." [1] Mr. Eliot finds that in " Hamlet " the " objective correla-

[1] " The Sacred Wood ", p. 100.

tive " is inadequate to the emotion it expresses ; that Hamlet feels a disgust for which the play provides no sufficient object. Mr. Eliot himself sometimes fails to make his external facts adequate to his disgust. It is not for want of trying ; hence the emphasis on the mean and squalid and the grating similes. Mr. Eliot may, indeed, seem to attach too snobbish an importance to the housemaid in the area and the toothbrush on the wall. He uses them as the " formula " of loathing ; but the formula does not evoke in his audience an equivalent loathing. Perhaps it was the difficulty of finding a sufficient object for disgust which led him later to a style largely symbolical. The lilac and the hyacinth speak to him of regret ; the nightingale sings of " adulterous wrong " ; the rat's foot it is that rattles the bones in the garret of humanity ; and so we come to a picture of perdition as simple and irrefutable as a nursery rhyme :

> Here we go round the prickly pear
> Prickly pear prickly pear
> Here we go round the prickly pear
> At five o'clock in the morning.

．　　．　　．　　．　　．　　．　　．

The quotations in this essay will have shown that there is some excuse for those who call Mr. Eliot a " modernist ". I hope they will also have shown that Mr. Eliot's allusive manner has its points. But when the allusive manner is carried to its extremes, when a passage of a score of lines becomes little more than a

mosaic of borrowings, the reader begins to question its
legitimacy. This may be plagiarism with a difference ;
but what is the difference ?

Concurrent with the idea of fusion is the idea of
continuity with the past. " We dwell with satisfaction
upon the poet's difference from his predecessors, especi-
ally his immediate predecessors ; we endeavour to find
something that can be isolated in order to be enjoyed.
Whereas if we approach a poet without this prejudice
we shall often find that not only the best, but the most
individual parts of his work may be those in which the
dead poets, his ancestors, assert their immortality most
vigorously ".[1] The poet, says Mr. Eliot, must feel his
responsibility towards the dead as well as towards the
living ; he must have the sense of tradition. But
tradition " cannot be inherited, and if you want it you
must obtain it by great labour. It involves, in the first
place, the historical sense, which we may call nearly
indispensable to anyone who would continue to be a
poet beyond his twenty-fifth year ; and the historical
sense involves a perception, not only of the pastness of
the past, but of its presence ; the historical sense compels a man to write not merely with his own generation
in his bones, but with a feeling that the whole of the
literature of Europe from Homer and within it the whole
of the literature of his own country has a simultaneous
existence and composes a simultaneous order ".[2] The
amount of learning needed in order to win a place in
the European tradition varies with the individual.

[1] " The Sacred Wood ", p. 48.   [2] Ibid., p. 49.

" Some can absorb knowledge, the more tardy must sweat for it. Shakespeare acquired more essential history from Plutarch than most men could from the whole British Museum." [1] But at least learning never comes amiss ; wanting it, the poet wants also that consciousness of unity with the past which forbids him to make his poetry merely the expression of his own personality. And so we come back to the analogy of the catalyst ; in the poet's mind are concentrated past and present, personal and borrowed ; what emerges is neither personal nor borrowed, but new. We begin to see why Mr. Eliot writes as if Webster were talking into one ear and the prophet Ezekiel into the other.

So far, then, from breaking away from tradition, Mr. Eliot clings to it ; and the very methods which seem most unorthodox are in intention the most " traditional ". Since he thinks it the poet's business to be conscious of the living past he has no scruples about advertising that consciousness ; he makes a point of plagiarism. And so in " Five-Finger Exercises " we find echoes of Shakespeare and Herrick, Tennyson and Edward Lear, Keats and Marvell and Alfred de Musset —a witticism with an undercurrent of seriousness. Most people suppose that a poet's mind is stocked with images. Mr. Eliot recommends stocking it with remembered phrases as well ; then, when the creative moment comes, Goldsmith and Shakespeare, St. Augustine and the writer of popular songs contribute each his fragment ; the result is not simply a collection of reminiscences, but

[1] " The Sacred Wood ", p. 52.

the expression of an emotion, a new thought. The emotion is " depersonalized ", since any personal element has been fused with the rest to make the new indivisible whole ; Mr. Eliot demands " emotion which has its life in the poem and not in the history of the poet ".[1] Edith Sitwell reacts against the nudity of the rustic Wordsworth tradition ; Mr. Eliot reacts against the lack of precision in the romantic tradition, its emphasis on personal emotion, above all its indifference to Authority.

Fusion and allusion ; the preservation of tradition by the study of the past ; the " depersonalization " of emotion—the theory explains the intention of the poetry even when it cannot elucidate its meaning. It is still possible to criticize the method, to say that tradition can be preserved without an elaborate system of quotations, and that Mr. Eliot has gone a long way round to establish communications with the past. Most open to criticism is the obscurity into which his theory leads him. It is, as I have said, obvious that Mr. Eliot prefers to be understood (though one suspects wilfulness when, passing over half the problems of " The Waste Land ", he stops to tell us in a note that the hermit thrush of line 357 is *Turdus aonalaschkae pallasii*). But by whom does he expect to be understood ? Does he suppose the average reader of poetry will understand the passage quoted on page 73, or see the joke when, in a parody of Day's " Parliament of Bees ", Actaeon and Diana are replaced by Sweeney and Mrs. Porter ?

[1] Ibid., p. 59.

Does he hope for the appreciation of posterity, and leave to the emendators of the future the task of grappling with a poet whom his contemporaries found incomprehensible ? It is true that the reader of to-day is often incorrigibly idle. We have been spoilt by the simplicity of the bulk of poetry for half a century ; but do we need quite such a lesson as Mr. Eliot gives us ?

Certainly there is respectable precedent for his methods. Plagiarism is common with poets ; Mr. Eliot points out a fine example of parody in Dryden, who took Cowley's lines beginning

> Where their vast courts the mother-waters keep

and wrote

> Where their vast courts the mother-strumpets keep.

One can no more understand Milton without an acquaintance with classical mythology than one can understand Mr. Eliot without an acquaintance with the work of Miss Jessie L. Weston. As for obscurity, the Elizabethans are not easy poets. Take, for instance, a passage from Tourneur's " Revenger's Tragedy " quoted by Mr. Eliot :

> And now methinks I could e'en chide myself
> For doating on her beauty, though her death
> Shall be revenged after no common action.
> Does the silkworm expend her yellow labours
> For thee ? For thee does she undo herself?
> Are lordships sold to maintain ladyships
> For the poor benefit of a bewildering minute ?

88

Why does yon fellow falsify highways,
And put his life between the judge's lips,
To refine such a thing—keeps horse and men
To beat their valours for her ?

It is no less difficult with its fusion of images and its
swift transitions of thought than the meditative passages
in the 1920 " Poems " ; and Mr. Lytton Strachey was
not far out when he linked " the profound obscurities
of Shakespeare and Mr. T. S. Eliot ". Mr. Eliot, however, is not content to let tradition speak for him.
" . . . It appears likely ", he declares, " that poets in
our civilization, as it exists at present, must be *difficult.*
Our civilization comprehends great variety and complexity, and this variety and complexity, playing upon
a refined sensibility, must produce various and complex results. The poet must become more and more
comprehensive, more allusive, more indirect, in order
to force, to dislocate if necessary, language into his
meaning." [1] This is an unexpected avowal from a
writer who has complained of the amount of criticism
" taken up with discussing whether, and in what degree,
this book or novel or poem is expressive of *our* mentality,
of the personality of our age ".   It is also an illuminating
avowal, since it implies that Mr. Eliot is resigned to
the prospect of being difficult. The poet must look,
he goes on to say, into more than the heart. " One
must look into the cerebral cortex, the nervous system,
and the digestive tracts." [2] Not all Mr. Eliot's surface

[1] " Homage to John Dryden ", p. 31.
[2] Ibid., p. 33.

oddities, then, need be put down to fusion or a feeling for tradition. He is determined to keep up with the present as well as with the past ; no wonder if the reader is bewildered by the variety of the material. Mr. Eliot once wrote of the plan of " Ulysses " : " It is simply a way of controlling, of ordering, of giving a shape and a significance to the immense panorama of futility and anarchy which is contemporary history." Similarly the plan of " The Waste Land " reduces to order Mr. Eliot's vision of a society which even in decay grows more and more complex ; at the same time the poem, by its incidental concentration of an enormous variety of experiences, reflects the complexity of that society. And so it is with Mr. Eliot's work ; ultimately the verse is difficult because it aims at giving as complete an expression as possible to a vast, confused, disintegrating civilization. The reader, then, must expect obscurities ; Mr. Eliot does not write for those who assume that art will be made easy for them. For a long time now literature has been democratic : that is to say, it has been regarded as the property of the people as a whole and not of the educated minority. Mr. Eliot reacts against this attitude. His poetry is essentially aristocratic, the appeal of a scholar and a wit to a small world of letters. And so we come to an idiom almost as incomprehensible to the general public as the Latin of the Middle Ages was to the contemporary masses.

. . . .

I have pointed to Mr. Eliot's use of discord and con-

trast ; and indeed it becomes increasingly clear that
here is to be found the key to the movement of his
mind. Is he not a man perpetually seeking harmony
amongst discords ? As a young man he is possessed
by violent aesthetic disgust. The sham culture of the
rich, the dingy pretences of the fringes of society, the
squalor of poverty,—wherever he looks he sees ugliness
and discord ; tormented, he escapes from

> The eyes that fix you in a formulated phrase,

only to be sickened by

> . . . such a vision of the street
> As the street hardly understands ;

But gradually a worse torment overtakes him. Aesthetic
disgust is succeeded by moral disgust ; Mr. Eliot becomes
intolerably aware of a vast spiritual rot underlying the
material squalor. Death is at the roots of society ; and
in an agonizing vision he sees the whole structure collapse into chaos. Life has resolved itself into a universal
discord.

Obviously Mr. Eliot's position was unendurable.
There was one way out—by submission to supernatural
authority. And in Christianity Mr. Eliot found a
means of reconciling the contrasts which had tortured
him. He " perceived that what really matters is Sin
and Redemption " ; he perceived that Christianity can
bridge the gulf between Pascal's infinites of greatness
and meanness. And so at last, driven by an excess of
loathing, he took refuge in the authority of the Church.
Henceforth a single emotion dominates his poetry.

The rumour of everyday life still provides a discordant accompaniment (though it is noticeable that as Mr. Eliot withdraws from the world he is inclined to find it less repellent) ; but all conflicting experiences and emotions are controlled by the desire for the divine peace. The 1925 " Poems " are the expression of a general view of civilization ; " Ash Wednesday " is in the main the expression of an individual experience. And so it is that the later verse (except, of necessity, " The Rock ") has a personal quality which is not found in the earlier.

Naturally the struggles by which Mr. Eliot achieves this harmony are reflected in his style. I have tried to show the importance in his theory of the idea of fusion —the fusion of disparate experiences, of past and present, of individual and general. But this after all is only an attempt at realizing harmony of expression, at reconciling the contrasts which are innate in the material of poetry. Indeed, as time goes on the discords grow less strident. Gradually we move out of a world full of jangling sounds and incoherent images ; gradually the nightmare of the early poems, a nightmare where

> Midnight shakes the memory
> As a madman shakes a dead geranium.

gives place to the clearer but no less terrible visions of daylight. Mr. Eliot is, as I have said, forcing his contrasts into an easily recognized relation ; and by the time we come to " The Waste Land " the discords have

been reduced by terrific concentration to a kind of
unwilling harmony. In " Ash Wednesday " the harmony is no longer unwilling. The concentration of
images and phrases is still apparent ; but the single
emotion which controls the sequence has called forth
a certain unity of expression. The borrowed fragments
have often a devotional or liturgical origin : " And after
this our exile " from the Salve Regina : " Lord, I am
not worthy . . . but speak the word only " from the
priest's private devotions in the Mass : " O my people,
what have I done unto thee " from the Reproaches in
the Mass of the Presanctified : " suffer me not to be
separated " from the Anima Christi. And the imagery
too—unicorns, junipers, the Rose, the Lady—gives the
verse a smoothness which is new in Mr. Eliot's work.
The unifying emotion thus shines out clearly ; it does
not emerge obscurely and with difficulty from a cloud
of contrasts. In the two later pieces, " Triumphal
March " and " Difficulties of a Statesman ", there is a
return to discord—even to discord identical with that
of the earlier poems : eagles, trumpets, crumpets.[1]
But it is used with a different purpose. The intention
is no longer to fuse disparate material, nor is it, as in
the earliest collection, to give an impression of squalor
and disintegration ; it is to show the single mind at
variance with the external world. For at last the belief
in the single mind which was lacking in the " Prufrock "
poems has been won ; there *is* " a still moment "

. . . Where the dove's foot rested and locked for a moment,

---

[1] Cf. p. 70.

Meanwhile in " Ash Wednesday " Mr. Eliot's poetic theory has coincided with his religious creed. Harmony has been achieved in both ; in both Authority—the authority of the European tradition, the authority of the Church—has been accepted. Tradition in poetry, tradition in religion—as Arnold Bennett once said. Mr. Eliot is American, but probably less so than any American now on earth ; he has become more European than the Europeans.

Like Lawrence, Mr. Eliot sees man being degraded by industrial civilization. But while Lawrence found salvation in submission to a physical authority, in the resurrection of the body and the life everlasting of sex, Mr. Eliot, shrinking from the physical, submits to an authority outside nature. Pity with him has been almost submerged in disgust ; he has never been able to accept the contradictions in humanity as they are, and life has no pattern for him until he can interpret his restlessness and his disgust as consciousness of sin. Once original sin has been recognized the way is clear ; it is the opposite way to Lawrence's. And while Lawrence is a moralist preaching salvation, Mr. Eliot is an individual primarily concerned with his own escape from unbearable sensibility. He has propounded no new remedy for the diseases of civilization ; we must look elsewhere to explain his importance to his generation.

First we must reckon with his historical importance. I shall try to show presently how the Sitwells, reacting against the sobriety into which the Wordsworth tradi-

tion has led recent verse, have reintroduced the element
of decoration, even of extravagant decoration, into
poetry. Mr. Eliot reverts, not to a decorative, baroque
tradition, but to an intellectual tradition. Mr. George
Williamson in " The Talent of T. S. Eliot " has laid
stress on Mr. Eliot's relation to Donne and the " metaphysical " school. Certainly we find in his poetry a
complexity of thought missing from English poetry since
the seventeenth century. We find also a precision of
thought which is a challenge to the Romantic tradition. But its close-packed quality, its intellectual concentration, does not exclude passion ; nor does it
exclude richness and individuality of expression. Much
has been written of Mr. Eliot's debt to the Symbolists.[1]
The Symbolists brought a new, violent, flashing life
into French poetry ; Mr. Eliot, diverting some of that
new life across the Channel, has used it to perfect an
idiom of his own. The clash of impressions, the ironic
juxtaposition of noble and vulgar, the kaleidoscopic
vision of a world composed of shifting, quarrelling fragments—certainly Mr. Eliot has brought a new manner
into English poetry. And when we add to these the
element of literary allusion we are faced with a style
which in complexity and concentration and *suggestive-
ness* has few rivals. Even the metres are unfamiliar.
Many of Mr. Eliot's poems are written in a strictly
orthodox four-line rhyming stanza. But there are many

[1] Cf. " Axel's Castle " by Edmund Wilson (Scribners) and an
article on " The Classicism of T. S. Eliot " by René Taupin (translated by Louis Zukofsky) in " The Symposium " (January, 1932).

others whose form refuses to be classified. We find irregular rhymed stanzas. We find a kind of *vers libre* into which assonances and repetitions and occasional rhymes have been introduced. We find blank verse stretched to accommodate so great a variety of rhythms that it almost ceases to be blank verse. Not only the style and the material but also the form is used to reflect the complications of modern society.

Like the prose of Joyce, Mr. Eliot's verse has been hailed as the beginning of a fresh development in literature. It is doubtful whether the idea of fusion and allusion can be carried much farther than Mr. Eliot has himself carried it. But there can be no doubt that his work is having its effect on English verse. Poetry is once again being used as the vehicle for satire and social criticism ; it is being used as the vehicle for austere thought. Much of the intellectual element in present-day poetry can be traced to the influence of Mr. Eliot. But, while reviving the " metaphysical " tradition, he has imposed on it a " symbolist " style. The compound is unique in English verse ; and it has inaugurated a movement towards seriousness, precision, sharpness : a movement never more needed than now.

But how, it may be asked, can so obscure a poetic style expect to survive, far less to propagate itself ? It is often argued that no poetry as difficult as Mr. Eliot's has been handed down from the past ; that literature in order to endure must be within the grasp of the average educated man, and that Mr. Eliot with every allusion to Kyd and the Upanishads condemns himself to a quicker eclipse. The answer to that is that the understanding of poetry depends largely on familiarity with its idiom. Among the generation now beginning to read and write poetry there are many who claim to find Mr. Eliot's work perfectly simple. That may be partly due to willingness to overlook the difficulties ; it is also due to the fact that, for the new generation, Mr. Eliot's idiom has lost some of its strangeness and at the same time much of its obscurity. To the next generation it may seem as natural as the Romantic idiom, which so much disturbed its first critics, seems to us. The allusions must remain a stumbling-block ; for in no age can the average educated man be supposed to be familiar with both Day's " Parliament of Bees " and the Buddha's Fire Sermon. It is possible that the allusive style may be modified to accommodate more readers. It is more likely that, as I have hinted, a new learned literature will run parallel to the vernacular writings of Mr. J. B. Priestley and Mr. John Masefield. To those for whom it is written the effort of mastering it will not appear too great ; people have after all been known not only to learn Greek, but also to look up the topical allusions in Aristophanes.

As for Mr. Eliot's work itself, its intrinsic value easily justifies the effort required to overcome its difficulties. First there is its astonishing scope. We have seen at what widely separated points it touches on literature ; how it fuses past and present ; how in its analysis of civilization it surveys all classes of society. Anthropology, history, philosophy, religion—it is long since poetry has embraced such a variety of subjects. The result is a synthesis of impressions which, to a generation obsessed with its own confusion, is peculiarly satisfying. And this mosaic of experiences and ideas gives an effect of richness and solidity which one had despaired of finding in the poetry of the beginning of this century. It gives also a feeling of excitement. In verse which makes use of such varied material the reader can never anticipate ; the sudden contrasts, the abrupt changes of tone, the concentration in fact of experiences which can be forced into relationship only by the poet himself, give an unfailing element of aesthetic surprise. The surprise, indeed, is almost excessive ; there are times when the use of contrast becomes a cliché. And yet one cannot help regretting that in some of the later poetry Mr. Eliot has used contrast far less freely. One misses the edge of the earlier verse, an edge which one repeatedly finds to be due to the impact of conflicting ideas. Mr. Eliot has rightly said that the " comic relief " in Shakespeare is " at its best an intensification of the sombreness " ; we have seen how in the same way his own " alliance of levity and seriousness " intensifies the seriousness. And if we look closely we see that not only the passages, but even the phrases which strike us as most pointed are often the result of a contrast.

> Branches of wistaria [*sic*]
> Circumscribe a golden grin ;
>
> But our lot crawls between dry ribs
> To keep our metaphysics warm.

Death and the Raven drift above
And Sweeney guards the horned gate.

But, contrast or no contrast, Mr. Eliot's phrases have
the precision, the aptness, the finality which are found
only in considerable poetry. Ultimately this genius for
the unquestionable phrase is more important than any
historical contribution. We remember Mr. Eliot's work
for its harsh contemptuous irony. We remember it for
lines which, without any violence of diction, sting like
a blow in the face :

. . . that woman
who hesitates toward you in the light of the door
which opens on her like a grin.

We remember it for the piercing melancholy of its
moments of regret. Most of all we remember it for
its sudden escapes from scorn and disgust, for the intensity of the phrases with which it suggests, even more
than it describes, an imagined or a recollected beauty :

. . . What will the spider do,
Suspend its operations, will the weevil
Delay ? De Bailhache, Fresca, Mrs. Cammel, whirled
Beyond the circuit of the shuddering Bear
In fractured atoms. Gull against the wind, in the windy
    straits
Of Belle Isle, or running on the Horn,
White feathers in the snow, the Gulf claims,
And an old man driven by the Trades
To a sleepy corner.

Mr. Eliot's work has not the qualities of size and space

and universality which we are accustomed to sum up loosely in the term " great " literature. But it is a form of expression which by its force and its justice continually shocks us into recognition of the unfamiliar ; which, in short, provides us with a new and powerful aesthetic experience. And that, after all, is what we call poetry.

EDITH SITWELL

EDITH SITWELL

The time when the name Sitwell could excite controversy is past ; the years since the War have brought into English poetry experiments beside which the Sitwellian contribution appears conservative ; and nowadays a serious critic can dismiss it as belonging " to the history of publicity rather than of poetry ".[1] The eclipse is partly due to a reaction against " poetic " writing. Younger authors have flung themselves into verse with, apparently, a savage contempt for its graces ; the tendency of poetry has been towards harshness, toughness, the obscure difficult motion. It is true that at the first impact Miss Sitwell's verse seemed harsh enough. But it was the harshness of light and not of obscurity ; harshness, moreover, juxtaposed with softness and fluidity ; clearly this was poetry decked, not poetry stripped. The real reason for the neglect of her work, however, goes deeper ; it is not aesthetic, but moral. It is becoming the fashion to regard poetry, not as existing by its own right, but as willingly conditioned by its social and political environment. " A

[1] " New Bearings in English Poetry ", by F. R. Leavis, p. 73 (Chatto & Windus).

103

poet cannot expect to write well, to give pleasure to his most careful critics," declares Mr. Michael Roberts, " unless he is abreast of his own times. . . ." [1] Steadily sympathy decreases for verse which holds itself apart from social and economic exigencies ; insidiously poetry is suborned for the ends of propaganda. Miss Sitwell is not indifferent to her own times. But her first care is for poetry ; and to the propagandist poetry is not enough. Her exotic imagery seems mere snobbery to a generation engrossed with the idea of the Marxist State ; her experiments with abstract pattern are pointless to an age crying out for moral conflict.

And yet moral conflict is one of the main themes of her earliest published work : that is to say of " The Mother " (1915) ; of " Twentieth Century Harlequinade " (with Osbert Sitwell, 1916) ; of her contributions to the first two volumes of the anthology " Wheels " (1916 and 1917). Already she is faced with the problem of treachery : the necessity of reconciling experience of infamy and death with conviction of good. She shows us Saul red-handed from the murder of his brother ; she writes of a mother killed by her son :

> They say the Dead may never dream.
> But yet I heard my pierced heart scream
> His name within the dark. They lie
> Who say the Dead can ever die.

But the tragedy, the abyss to which she points, is not only physical dissolution ; it is also the rot in the spirit

---

[1] Preface to " New Signatures ", p. 8 (Hogarth Press).

which ends in the extinction of the soul. The traitor, the murderer it is who dies. The death-theme is simply stated ; it has none of the elaboration which we shall meet in her later work. The interesting thing is that it is stated so early. For spiritual death supplies the central conflict of her poetry ; this is the discord which she is called on to resolve into harmony. When she first faces it she can see nothing but disintegration as the outcome : " souls that die " ; the disintegration that belongs to darkness, the tomb and its worms, " those slow mean servitors ". But she is confronted, too, with another kind of spiritual death ; the death that belongs to light and aridity. Hence the second of the early themes, the vision of Vanity Fair ; a city of blind houses and dusty booths where

> The busy chatter of the heat
> Shrilled like a parokeet ;

Miss Sitwell is apt to regard the more urban amusements of mankind with asperity ; at first when she wants to indict the inanity of modern civilization she describes a fashionable concert or a seaside resort with its kaleidoscope of colour, its " noisy light ", its Bank Holiday crowds, " bright sparks struck out by Time ". But she needs symbolical figures for her Vanity Fair ; she needs a setting less localized than the esplanade, more sinister in its gaiety than the Fun Fair. She finds what she wants in the Commedia dell'arte ; in its glittering, grotesque characters, masked and faintly diabolical ; in its fantastic clowning ; above all in its

105

wilful departure from the natural. And so by 1918, the date of " Clown's Houses " and the third volume of " Wheels ", she is developing the idea of the harlequinade—a harlequinade staged in the airless streets of hell. She is still developing it in the 1919 and 1920 " Wheels " and in " The Wooden Pegasus " (1920). Pantaloon and Scaramouche play together in the " spangled weather " ; Brighella chatters and scolds ; Il Dottore sits in his " rickety top story "

> While an ape, with black spangled veil,
> Plum'd head-dress, face dust-pale,
> Scratch'd with a finger-nail
>
> Sounds from a mandoline,
> Tuneless and sharp as sin :—

Again and again in her poetry we meet the Commedia dell'arte figures : Harlequin, Il Magnifico, Il Capitaneo, Pierrot, Columbine. Sometimes the puppet-show takes the place of the harlequinade ; sometimes a passage is reminiscent of the Russian ballet ; always she uses her material to give the effect of hard garish light, jangling sound and an infinite spiritual desolation.

About the time when Miss Sitwell was first introducing the posturing figures of the Italian Comedy into her poetry another type of character was also making its appearance. While Pantaloon and Brighella are skirmishing among the " puppet booths " of hell, Silenus is pilfering the plums in the Deanery garden, and satyrs and naiads are heard laughing between the strawberry beds. The foundations, in fact, of a bucolic

style are being laid, and in 1923 a volume of verse is
published with the name " Bucolic Comedies ". Miss
Sitwell's earliest bucolics are often concerned with what
she has herself called " the animal state of consciousness,
shaping itself from within, beginning to evolve shape
out of its thick black blot of darkness " [1]

> (Queer impulses of bestial kind,
> Flesh indivisible from mind.)

She writes of the puppet fumbling for speech :

> Yet dust bears seeds that grow to grace
> Behind my crude-striped wooden face

> As I, a puppet tinsel-pink,
> Leap on my springs, learn how to think,

or of the ape dimly aware

> That narrow long Eternity

> Is but the whip's lash o'er our eyes—
> Spurring to new vitalities.

And throughout, behind the gaiety of the bucolic scene,
behind the frolics of dairymaid and gardener, goosegirl
and satyr, there lurks the menace of " a terrible groping
animal consciousness " [2] : the unknown menace of darkness to light, nightmare to dream. The countryside is

[1] " Experiment in Poetry ", an essay published in " Tradition
and Experiment in Present-Day Literature," p. 87 (Oxford University Press).
[2] " Tradition and Experiment in Present-Day Literature ", p. 90.

no longer the cricketer's paradise of Georgian verse. It is a region where the spirit is numbed, where

> . . . country gentlemen
> Took flying Psyche for a hen
> And aimed at her ;

where a monstrous artificial aristocracy lives embalmed in " endless vacancy of mind ". In this society the only *aubade* is that sung to the drudge who comes down in the " creaking empty light " to kindle

> Flames as staring, red and white,
>
> As carrots or as turnips,

Familiar fairy-tales grow sinister ; the witch sends the girl to the well, and as she fills her pail the water hops and whimpers in uncouth entreaty. Nature itself is threatening :

> The curé-black leaves
> Are cawing like a rook . . .

or else enveloped in huge snowy grief ; or, sometimes, informed by a mocking sensuality. And the fragments of personal experience embedded in the bucolics deepen the impression of melancholy. These sketches of child-hood bring with them an elegance foreign to the animal heaviness of many of the " comedies " ; but it is the elegance of the irrevocable. The child walks in a landscape now faded ; and even as she walks there is heard from the branches the fluttering of a primitive consciousness—the " Beginnings of first earthy things ! "

From the start Miss Sitwell showed a gift for nursery rhyme and nonsense verse, and before long she was using this gift to make elaborate experiments in "texture" and metre. She was writing verses labelled "Foxtrot" or "Hornpipe"; she was writing a new version of "I do Like to be Beside the Seaside";

When
                    Don
Pasquito arrived at the seaside
Where the donkey's hide tide brayed, he
Saw the banditto Jo in a black cape
Whose slack shape waved like the sea—
Thetis wrote a treatise noting wheat is silver like the
    sea; the lovely cheat is sweet as foam; Erotis
    notices that she
                Will
                Steal
                The
Wheat-king's luggage, like Babel
Before the League of Nations grew—
So Jo put the luggage and the label
In the pocket of Flo the Kangaroo.

She prefixes to "Façade" (1922), in which a number of these experimental verses are collected, an extract from one of her own essays: "This modern world is but a thin match-board flooring spread over a shallow hell. For Dante's hell has faded, is dead. Hell is no vastness; here are no more devils who laugh or who weep—only the maimed dwarfs of this life, terrible straining mechanisms, crouching in trivial sands, and laughing at the giants' crumbling!" And, indeed, when we come to look closely at these apparent jingles, they have no real light-heartedness. Something of the acerbity which informs her view of our English Lidos has crept into her rendering of the popular song too ; the metrical gaiety is the " façade " of an interior gloom. " In those poems ", she writes, " which deal with the world crumbling to dust, with materialism building monstrous shapes out of the deadened dust, I, for one, use the most complicated dance rhythms which could be found, or else syncopated rhythms which are not dance rhythms." [1] " Materialism building monstrous shapes out of the deadened dust "—that is a plain enough indication of the significance of many experimental poems. Miss Sitwell believes that the machine age is " mirrored in modern syncopated dance music " ; and she believes that poetry, to be expressive of " the world crumbling to dust ", must have rhythms as violent.[2]

And so in " Façade " the verse at times seems to run berserk. But it is the calculated insanity of a machine. The rhythms jerk and plunge, but always inside the limits of a steely pattern ; a word, a sound is tossed up, vanishes and reappears with the regularity of a piston. " Trio for Two Cats and a Trombone " : " Lullaby for Jumbo " : " When Sir Beelzebub "—the titles have an air of high spirits which is misleading.

[1] " Tradition and Experiment in Present-Day Literature ", p. 76.
[2] Cf. Mr. Eliot's suggestion " that poets in our civilization, as it exists at present, must be *difficult* " (see p. 89).

For much as Miss Sitwell may enjoy her own experiments, the laughter in these high-speed pieces is always faintly demoniacal. Half-frightful, half-ludicrous, like the creatures of folk-lore, the figures in the dance grimace and gibber—King Pompey the emperor's ape ; Black Mrs. Behemoth ; the snoring Noctambulo ; Ass-Face ; " the navy-blue ghost of Mr. Belaker " peering in at the window ; Heliogabalusene the Bat hanging head down

> Near the Castle wall of the ultimate Shade
> Where decoy duck dust
> Quacks, clacks, afraid.

When for a moment the pace slackens it is to admit the lumbering forms of " animal consciousness " ; fire " furry as a bear " ; the spirit that

> . . . grieves
> In the torrid day ?

Only occasionally in " Façade " does Miss Sitwell use her virtuosity with gentler effect : to mimick the owl or recall the melancholy of fading snow.

So far she has not found much solace in a world " crumbling to dust ". Treachery and spiritual decay have opened a gulf at her feet. Society has declared itself the modern Vanity Fair. The English countryside has proved bucolic beyond endurance. In the present there seems no haven for this acute and irritable mind ; there remains the past. And in the past she finds the elegance, the grace, the soft civilized beauty which she vainly seeks in the present. It is to her own childhood that she turns for solace, to days when

> . . . life still held some promise,—never ask
> Of what,—but life seemed less a stranger, then,
> Than ever after in this cold existence.

And in " The Sleeping Beauty " (1924) and " Troy Park " (1925) she looks back to the dreaming summers of youth. " The Sleeping Beauty " is a revised version of the fairy-tale ; " Troy Park " when it first appeared contained a number of poems which in the " Collected Poems " are included with " Façade " and the " Bucolic Comedies ". But the " Troy Park " of the collected edition is almost entirely autobiographical. Both fairy-tale and reminiscence have the same landscape ; Troy Park (according to Mr. Megroz the name of a real place) [1] is identified with Renishaw Park, the home of Miss Sitwell as a child ; it is also merged in the park of the Sleeping Princess. And there, within the walls of the " sweet and ancient gardens " which were the Eden of an innocent age, singing birds forever move

> Among the boughs with silent feathered feet,—
> Spraying down dew like jewels amid the sweet
>
> Green darkness ;

nereids haunt the " green deep mirrors " of the lake ; leaves " breasted like a dove " murmur romantic tales,

[1] Mr. R. L. Megroz's book " The Three Sitwells " (Richards Press, 1927) contains useful biographical information.

and the moonlight tells of " Circean enchantments and far seas ". All day the child wanders with her brothers in " an hallucination born of silence " ; time passes " suavely, imperceptibly ", undarkened as yet by the menace of death.

> Life was so beautiful that shadow meant
> Not death, but only peace, a lovely lulling.

But outside the walls the menace waits ; death and betrayal are in ambush. And so no Prince comes to break through the " brutish forests " and entice Miss Sitwell's Sleeping Beauty from her safe castle grounds.

> " And oh, far best," the gardener said,
> " Like fruits to lie in your kind bed,—
> To sleep as snug as in the grave
> In your kind bed, and shun the wave,
> Nor ever sigh for a strange land
> And songs no heart can understand."

The Princess is left to sleep on in her enchanted forest ; the fairy-tale at least must have a happy ending. But this is a wish fulfilled only in dream ; in actuality the outcome is different. Already for the child " the darkening shadow " creeps nearer ; a moment of thoughtless cruelty warns her that

> Cold Death had taken his first citadel.

And one day there is a crisis.

> And all the mad Cassandra tongues of birds
> Cried " Troy is burning "—there, outside the window.—

An unexplained crisis ; but enough is implied for us to understand that time and treachery have irreparably breached the walls of Troy Park.

Miss Sitwell, it may be seen, has a personal quarrel with the present, since it has brought a decline from her experience of the past ; but, like almost every serious poet now writing, she sees also an historical decline (though this distresses her less). A general feeling of regret for the past finds expression in " Prelude to a Fairy Tale " (1927) and " Elegy on Dead Fashion " (1926). " Prelude to a Fairy Tale " gives us some characteristic Sitwellian mythology—Marshal Mars with the gout, Vulcan whiskered like Good Prince Albert. It also takes us back to an earlier theme— the theme of an evolving consciousness. But this time it is not merely an animal consciousness, but a consciousness growing from stone to plant, from plant to beast, from beast to man. In the first published version of the " Prelude " Miss Sitwell's theory of evolution affords some defence against the eternal menace of dissolution :

The death of fire is but the birth of air,

But in the " Collected Poems " this passage has been excised ; the " old world's black renown " shouts down " life's serenade ". And in " Elegy on Dead Fashion " we are reminded that evolution may work downwards as well as upwards. From a rococo lament for " elegances lost and fled ", for the fashion-plate nymphs of the 1840's, who

Walked beside the stream's drake-plumaged waters
In crinolines of plaided sarsenet,
Scotch caps, where those drake-curling waters wet

Their elegant insteps.—

for days when

Queen Thetis wore pelisses of tissue
Of marine blue or violet, or deep blue,
Beside the softest flower-bells of the seas.

Miss Sitwell goes on by an extravagant transition to
mourn the " ancient time of our primeval innocence ".
The nymphs are dead ; and now

They engineer great wells into the Styx
And build hotels upon the peaks of seas
Where the small trivial Dead can sit and freeze.

Psyche has become a kitchen-maid ; the gods are
" Time-crumbled into marionettes ". Death indeed is
to be feared and the " unreasoning grave " with its
" mountain-high forgetfulness " ; but

There are a thousand deaths the spirit dies
Unknown to the sad Dead that we despise.

And so once more we come to the theme of spiritual
decay. The years which destroy the dreams of childhood destroy also the integrity of the soul :

Age shrinks our hearts to ape-like dust . . . that ape
Looks through the eyes where all death's chasms gape

Between ourselves and what we used to be.

And in " Metamorphosis " (1928) Time, not Death,
plays Iago, Time bringing with it

> . . . that metamorphosis,
>
> When the appalling lion-claws of age
> With talons tear the cheek and heart, yet rage
>
> For life devours the bone, a tigerish fire ?

But in this, the noblest of her poems, Miss Sitwell re-
states the evolution motive. And suddenly it takes on
sureness and significance : sureness, since it revivifies
instead of threatening her poetry ; significance, since
it is recognized as the solution to the problems of age
and death.

> And from the amber dust that was a rose
> In the green heat Parthenope still grows.

For the first time there is an absolute certainty in her
work. The certainty of technique has been present
from the beginning ; an interior certainty is now
added ; faith in poetry is reinforced by faith in the
unbroken rhythm of life. The discord of death has
been resolved into harmony. And " animal consciousness " is no longer a menace ; it has become part of
the universal unfolding of death into life :

> Since all things have beginnings ; the bright plume
> Was once thin grass in shady winter's gloom
>
> And the furred fire is barking for the shape
> Of hoarse-voiced animals ; cold air agape
>
> Whines to be shut in water's shape and plumes ;

" Metamorphosis " thus provides the counterpart to the
" Bucolic Comedies " ; and it unites and clarifies the
principal themes of " Prelude to a Fairy Tale " and
" Elegy on Dead Fashion ". When in 1933 it is reprinted, together with the " Elegy " and three new
poems, under the title " Five Variations on a Theme ",
Miss Sitwell has nothing fresh to add. The three
additional variations, " Romance " and two " Songs ",
do no more than refine the melancholy implicit in a
theme so delicately balanced between life and death.

In the poetry with which I have so far been dealing
she has always shown herself at war with the present.
But her hatred has been only vaguely orientated. And
the quarrel, as I have implied, is more personal than
general ; even when, as in the " Prelude " and the
" Elegy ", her work is the expression rather of belief
than of experience, private bitterness is never far away.
In 1929, however, she makes a devastating excursion
into satire, and ranges herself uncompromisingly on the
side of the critics of society. " Gold Coast Customs "
is directed against a civilization which countenances
both the slum and the " cannibal mart " of fashionable
life. Driven by an indignation comparable with
Swift's, she identifies modern society with the negro
culture of Central Africa. It is here in our midst that
Munza, king of the cannibal Monbuttoo, " rattles his
bones in the dust ", here that the drums beat and the
fetiches screech " as they feel the slaves' spilt blood " ;
the Amazon Queen, masked and eyeless, pounding her
own child's bones in a mortar, is none other than Lady

Bamburgher, Society hostess. Miss Sitwell uses all the resources of her technique to communicate horror and loathing. The imagery is lurid as a nightmare ; the words grate unendurably :

> Like monkey skin
> Is the sea—one sin
> Like a weasel is nailed to bleach on the rocks
> Where the eyeless mud screeched fawning,

In fury and sustained invective the poem is unequalled in contemporary verse ; had she written nothing else it should have won her recognition as a serious poet. But in the midst of the general satire the personal note is heard ; not only humanity, but also the single heart is betrayed. And in two new elegies published in the " Collected Poems " (1930) treachery is still the theme. Ultimately, I think, the mainspring of all her work is rage against the powers which besieged Troy Park and reduced it. Clearly the poetry proceeds from an acute aesthetic sensibility. But behind aesthetic sensibility is a personal sensibility. Miss Sitwell never escapes from it for long. She does not even try to escape. For her instinct is to move, not forward, but back ; to return to the years before her vulnerable sensibility was wounded. The problem of time and death may have been solved for her ; the death of the spirit always remains a discord. And the only refuge from that discord lies in the past.

. . . .

In speaking of the subjects with which Miss Sitwell deals I have mentioned certain of her stage figures :

her marionettes and her clowns, the satyrs who, with their complementary naiads, sylphs and ondines, infest her groves and streams. It may be worth while to catalogue some of her stage properties too, since these play an important part in her poetry, and since, indeed, stage properties are always important when, as now, poetic diction is in a state of flux.

In one of the early poems there is a passage obviously imitated from " Goblin Market " ; and throughout her work Miss Sitwell uses the names of fruits much as Christina Rossetti or Andrew Marvell used them. Nectarines and apricots ; plums, apples and cherries ; figs, grapes, melons, strawberries—on walled garden, orchard and hot-house she levies toll. But Troy Park had a vegetable garden too, and so gherkins, cucumbers, aubergines and marrows play their part in this Sitwellian harvest festival. The flowers, again, are for the most part such as might have grown in Troy Park. Calceolarias, zinnias, fuchsias, marigolds, cinerarias, auriculas, primulas, snapdragons, dahlias, ranunculi, narcissi, carnations, stephanotis—certainly they are a change from the untutored primrose and daffodil and lesser celandine. In her use of both flowers and fruits we see Miss Sitwell attempting a richly decorated form of verse which is a challenge to the almost embarrassingly nude forms of the Georgians. The porphyry and amber, the jacynth, jasper and topaz which glimmer in her poetry are as much a challenge. Even her musical instruments are exotic ; the lute and the flute, it is true, are common to romantic poets, but her mandoline has a sophisticated, *fin-de-siècle* note, while the *chapeau chinois* is pure rococo. And in her decorative use of names she returns to a tradition almost extinguished since Swinburne. Certain names have a special attraction for her : names, such as Midas and Thetis, gold or silver in their associations as well as in their sound. But Miss Sitwell has names for every mood. Don Pasquito and Mr. Belaker, Heliogabalusene and Mrs. Behemoth ; Susan and Polly and Jane ; Helen, Deirdre, Semiramis, Cassandra ; Lady Immoraline, Myrrhine, Laidronette, Miss Pekoe, Miss Nettybun ; Malibran, Tamburini, Taglioni, Grisi—real or invented, they pour out inexhaustibly. And these personages are often rigged out in the most peculiar clothing. " Queen Thetis ", as we have seen, wears a pelisse ; Cupid has put on " white nankin trousers and a flat Scotch bonnet " ; Venus, decently wrapped in a shawl, drives by in her barouche ; while the Bacchantes have bought mittens. This is an early Victorian revival with a vengeance ; so Victorian that even the satyrs dance " the galloppade and the mazurka, Cracoviak, cachucha, and the turka ". And a baroque revival—with the peculiarity that the motives are as often derived from the 1840's as from the classics ; Balmoral takes the place of Olympus.

The use of adjectives is interesting. First one notices the way in which epithets normally reserved for one of the senses are extended to another. Not the wind, but the dew is " whining " ; the light is " creaking " or " squealing " ; flowers are " trilling ", breezes " nach-

reous ", " wrinkled " or " withered ", winds " pig-
snouted ". " The modernist poet's brain ", Miss Sitwell explains, " is becoming a central sense, interpreting
and controlling the other five senses. . . . His senses
have become broadened and cosmopolitanized ; they
are no longer little islands, speaking only their own
narrow language, living their sleepy life alone. When
the speech of one sense is insufficient to convey his entire
meaning, he uses the language of another." [1] So far,
so good ; but we are taken farther. A candle is " lollop-
ing galloping " ; dust is " decoy-duck " or " monkey-
skin black and white striped " ; mud is at once " eyeless ", " sightless ", " fawning ", " painted " and " giggling ". This is what Mr. Robert Graves calls the
" free-associative " method [2] ; ideas and images may
be related, not by logic, but by some chance association
in the poet's mind—in fact, by caprice. The language
of poetry is thus extended in Miss Sitwell's work, firstly
by the breakdown of the sense barricades, secondly by
the scaling of the ramparts of logic. She presses her
attack at one point in particular.

> I always was a little outside life,—
> And so the things we touch could comfort me ;

she writes of herself as a child ; a highly developed
sense of touch makes her constantly use adjectives of
surface. Woods are " bear-furred ", leaves " green
baize " ; a pool is " swanskin ", grass " beaver-

[1] " Poetry and Criticism ", p. 18 (1925) (Hogarth Press).
[2] " Contemporary Techniques of Poetry ", p. 41 (Hogarth Press).

smooth " ; the marrow has " dogskin " flowers ; a country house is " quilted red satin " ; the sea is " smooth black lacquer ". The last phrase shows yet another peculiarity of her style—her trick of comparing the natural thing with the artificial. The leaves, she says, are like green baize ; she does not say the green baize is like leaves.

> Like a still-room maid's yellow print gown
> Are the glazed chintz buttercups of summer

And we find seas that are " gilt rococo ", trees that " resemble a great pelerine ", a farm-pond " smooth as a daguerreotype ". The result is to make her poetry seem itself more artificial and sophisticated. But, as her stage properties show, it is not the sophistication which uses " prosaic " material for poetry, not the sophistication of Carlos Williams or the later E. E. Cummings. " That gold-fingered arborist, the wind " ; " branches gold-mosaic'd as the wave " ; " porphyry bones of nymphs whence grew the rose " : on every page some phrase proclaims the artificial poet. Miss Sitwell's vocabulary is definitely " poetic " ; it is not, as with many modern poets, the language of the navvy or the stockbroker.

I have already mentioned her experimental verses, the " foxtrots " and " hornpipes ", the " polkas " and " mazurkas " and " waltzes " in which she shows her virtuosity. Indeed, when one looks at her work as a whole one finds in it an astonishing variety of metres. The heroic couplet, the octosyllabic couplet, blank verse,

rhyming quatrains of two-, four- or five-stressed lines
are all here ; and here too is a quantity of verse as
variable from stanza to stanza as " Kubla Khan " or
" Goblin Market ". Often, as in her " foxtrots " and
" mazurkas ", she patents her own metres ; caprice or
the echo of a syncopated tune alone could be responsible
for the form of " Trio for Two Cats and a Trombone "—

> Long steel grass—
> The white soldiers pass—
> The light is braying like an ass.
> See
> The tall Spanish jade
> With hair black as nightshade
> Worn as a cockade !

Not only the metrical framework of these experimental
poems is peculiar, but also their internal pattern. In
her essay on " Poetry and Criticism " she refers (p. 22)
to " the habit of forming abstract patterns in words " :

> Said Il Magnifico
> Pulling a fico—
> With a stoccado
> And a gambado,
> Making a wry
> Face : " This corraceous
> Round orchidaceous
> Laceous porraceous
> Fruit is a lie ! "

The pattern of those words (from " Façade ") is nothing if not abstract ; as Mr. Graves and Miss Riding
remark, they defeat the best dictionary in the end.[1]

[1] " A Survey of Modernist Poetry ", p. 233 (Heinemann).

But though verse such as this may be logically unintelligible, it is still significant ; it communicates a mood of acrid mockery which logic might fail to convey. Miss Sitwell, however, is still more concerned with rhythm and " texture " than with " abstract patterns " (even with verse she must satisfy her sense of touch). And so we find throughout her work a subtle variation of movement and, to pursue the " touch " metaphor, of surface. She experiments with internal rhymes and assonances, with near-assonances and dissonances and alliteration, with " the different effect that two one-syllabled words and one two-syllabled word have on rhythm in heightening or slowing the speed ".[1] She tries to give the effect of a drowsy fire :

> The purring fire has a bear's dull fur,

or the chill of early spring :

> The wooden châlets of the cloud
> Hang down their dull blunt ropes to shroud
>
> Red crystal bells upon each bough

or the ghostly presence of the moonlight :

> Hours passed ; the soft melodious moonlight grows . . .
> A murmurous sound of far-off Circean seas
> And old enchantments and the growth of trees.

And we have seen to what grim purpose she can use her technique in " Gold Coast Customs ". Always she is inspired by a passionate care for the craftsmanship

---

[1] " Tradition and Experiment in Present-Day Literature ", p. 76.

of poetry. A self-conscious sophisticated writer, she
submits easily to its discipline ; she benefits by the
necessity of shaping and re-shaping her lines. Lawrence, a great *natural* writer, is uneasy under discipline ;
we have seen how, when he renders the same idea in
prose and in verse, what is direct and vivid in the prose
is apt to become blurred and cumbrous in the verse.
With Miss Sitwell it is just the opposite. The exigencies
of verse clarify her ideas, which in prose are often
incoherent and repetitive ; the same image gains in
the verse a richness and a delicacy wanting in the prose.
This passage, for example : " Yet what, I asked myself, would they do if they were confronted suddenly
with the realities which have been served up for them
like exotic fruits ? They would be terrified as a negro
king seeing for the first time the delicate, the evanescent,
the so-unexplainable and untouchable snow. They
would be struck silent by the cold of the spirit, that is
not like the cold of any winter they have known " [1]
—becomes in verse :

> What would these ghosts do, if the truths they know,
> That were served up like snow-cold jewelled fruits,
> And the enfeathered airs of lutes,
> Could be their guests in cold reality ?
> They would be shivering,
> Wide-eyed as a negro king
> Seeing the evanescent mirage snow,—
> They would be silenced by the cold
> That is of the spirit, endlessly,
> Unfabled, and untold.

---

[1] " The New Age ", July 20th, 1922.

The theme is automatically pitched higher ; the verse rhythm points the smooth phrases ; and the formality of the medium demands the elaborate diction in which Miss Sitwell is most at home.

. . . .

What then is the general effect of Miss Sitwell's poetry, of her bizarre mixture of satire and fantasy, " modernism " and tradition ? It is certainly a strange world through which she guides us. It is a world where betrayal is the common lot of the heart and where the triviality of existence frets the generous spirit into a travesty of itself. Civilization, in this Sitwellian land-scape, is rotting away ; gods and heroes are vanished, and a race of dwarfs gropes in the twilight of materialism. Where the business of everyday life goes on it is pursued with heartless and terrifying gaiety ; under a brazen sky the crowds laugh and play like creatures conscious of doom, while in their booths puppets ape the petty vices and bickerings of their masters. Over the country-side a sodden stupidity broods. But " animal con-sciousness ", perpetually struggling towards the light— the fire muttering with the voice of the beast, the beast claiming blood-kinship with the man—creates the feel-ing of a vague dark menace ; while man sinks the animal rises to mock him. Even when the menace is softened, even when death is, not defeated, but accepted, the terror of spiritual disintegration still encompasses him.

Except in one enchanted spot, which Miss Sitwell has called Troy Park. Within those walls it is always

summer. There the nightingale sings, not of Philo-
mela's grief, but of her youth before she learned dis-
honour ; innocence can never be deflowered in Troy
Park, since it is eternally the garden of childhood, the
garden where Beauty still dreams. Indeed, over the
whole garden with its shining fruits and bright flowers
there hovers the air of a dream. Miss Sitwell often
draws her themes from fairy-tales or folk-lore ; I am
inclined to think it is because there she finds just the
inconsequence, the distortion, the refracted light of the
visions of sleep. The whole of her work gives the effect
of a dream-scene. Her shrieking clowns and painted
puppets with their nightmarish laughter ; her satyrs and
sylphs and ondines, appearing and vanishing like images
between sleep and waking ; her wealth of names—
Queen Victoria rubbing shoulders with Captain Fra-
casse, Pharaoh with Miss Nettybun, Absolam with Sir
Rotherham Redde in just such a fantastic jumble as one
remembers after a troubled night—these are all figures
in the landscape of a dream. And Miss Sitwell's technique, her imagery and diction strengthen the impression of unreality. They transport us to a topsy-turvy
existence where we can see the wind, hear the light,
feel the sky. The elements of the scene have acquired
surprising qualities ; the sea is " castanetted ", the grass
is " cackling " and the waterfalls are " goat-footed ".
Woods and water grow furred and feathered ; and
through this bewildering landscape, where the fruit and
the flowers have the richness of an opium-eater's visions,
glide the exotic forms of Venus, Thetis and Panope

clad in the fashions of 1843. The very leaves turn tartan in sympathy.

We have, then, a succession of dream-pictures of which the supreme nightmare is Society with its obscene gaiety, " bunches of nerves that dance ". Across the field of our vision there dart incessantly groups of words that form and re-form themselves into patterns and for the moment obscure the object at which we were looking. And this panorama, this poetic cinematograph, is accompanied by the rhythm of a swiftly changing metre to which the characters of the piece jig and posture with lunatic agility. Yet at the centre of the hubbub there remains one tranquil spot. And this spot Miss Sitwell in spirit still inhabits. She has never really left Troy Park ; or, if from time to time she has left it, the brutality and treachery without drove her hastily back. So, living herself within the veil of a dream, the dream which was her own childhood, she looks out at the external world and sees that, too, as a dream. Her view of life remains in essence that of a child, a sensitive child seeing everything in terms of its own private world. Certainly the child is highly sophisticated ; for Miss Sitwell during her sallies into the public world has acquired armour and weapons. But beneath the sophistication the core of sensitiveness persists ; and this combination of the vulnerable and the well-defended it is that makes her retorts to her critics so ferocious.

It remains to consider her place in the development of English verse. Has she a place at all or is she outside tradition and incapable of any influence on the main stream of our poetry? Her first book was published in 1915. The War was only in its second year; the feeling that this was less a war for an ideal than a massacre had scarcely taken hold of the combatants. And if disillusion had not yet undermined the bases of assurance, if the tradition of patriotism and national confidence was still unshaken and the belief in the institutions of society still firm, how much more stable seemed the subjects and forms of verse! The Imagists had made little impression. Masefield, it is true, had introduced into a poem about a drunkard language more commonly associated with the Old Kent Road than with poetry. But for the most part English verse was still under the influence of the Wordsworth tradition, a tradition by now so much weakened as to be valueless. The new voices in French verse had awakened little echo on this side of the Channel, though here and there some genuine artist such as Flecker would declare that we were years behind the times. Rupert Brooke, W. H. Davies, Wilfrid Gibson—the anthology poets were nearly all "traditionalists". And one of the most discouraging features of the tradition was its soberness. Poetry had been stripped of decoration. Rhetoric no longer had a place in English verse.

Into this rustic vacuum the Sitwells suddenly flung their unicorns and their nymphs, their bright metallic landscapes and tinsel harlequinades. I do not say that their example was the most powerful in the years of literary experiment which followed. I do not even say that their direct influence was considerable. But I do believe that the emphasis on decoration, on rhetoric in their own work restored to English verse the possibility of a richness it seemed to have lost. Their disciples may not have been numerous ; but at least the Sitwell example had put back into people's heads the idea that verse might be decorative, rhetorical, sophisticated. Afterwards we find English poetry gradually assuming a new vigour and a new luxuriance, reaching out to fresh scenes and subjects and methods ; we find, in short, a poetic renaissance. The Sitwells have been only one of the forces which have gone to produce the renaissance ; but their share in it has been generous. And of the three Sitwells Edith with her courage and her energy has been by far the most effective.

A literary movement which begins as a revolt against a convention usually ends by stiffening into a convention of its own. Miss Sitwell has since 1915 been in the van of a mutinous army (though it is important to note that she is just as ready to lead the way back to an old servitude, to the pastoral formulæ of the seventeenth century or the dream-formulæ of the French Symbolists as to advance to a new " freedom"). And yet in her own work the beginning of authority is visible. I have referred to the part played by caprice in her relation of ideas and images. But when apparently incongruous ideas and images are related not once but again and again, when dust is repeatedly " decoy-duck ", when waves and waterfalls are persistently " goatish " or " goat-footed ", we are justified in suspecting that caprice is giving way to some kind of a system. And the consistent transfer of adjectives from the sphere of one sense to that of another steadily builds up the system. The reader begins to expect dew to " trill " and grass to " cackle " ; he begins to take it for granted that the fire will be " furry " and the breeze " pig-snouted ". He learns to feel at home in a landscape where skies that once were a familiar azure have grown " hairy ", where the foliage is " tartan ", the rain " guinea-fowl-plumaged " and the sun a " blackamoor ". Miss Sitwell's habit of repeating, not merely epithets and images, but also whole passages reinforces the evidence for authority. Certain themes recur with regularity.

> I was a member of a family
> Whose legend was of hunting—(all the rare
> And unattainable brightness of the air)—
> A race whose fabled skill in falconry
> Was used on the small song-birds and a winged
> And blinded Destiny . . .

This passage from " Troy Park " is found almost word for word in a prose essay published in " The New Age " in 1922 [1] ; it is echoed in " Bucolic Comedies " and in " The Sleeping Beauty ". It is extended in another passage from " The Sleeping Beauty " :

[1] This essay, and much of the verse, is reminiscent of Rimbaud, by whom Miss Sitwell has been strongly influenced. See her " Arthur Rimbaud—an Essay " in " Prose Poems from ' Les Illuminations ' ", put into English by Helen Rootham (1932 : Faber & Faber).

But country gentlemen who from their birth,
Like kind red strawberries, root deep in earth
And sleep as in the grave, dream far beyond
The sensual aspects of the hairy sky
That something hides, they have forgotten why !
And so they wander, aiming with their gun
At mocking feathered creatures that have learnt
That movement is but groping into life,—

which is in its turn reproduced in " Poetry and Criticism ". (A slightly different version of the prose is prefixed to " Bucolic Comedies ".) The motive of the country gentlemen rooted in their own gardens and groves recurs in " The Sleeping Beauty " and in " Bucolic Comedies " ; the motive of the degraded Destiny recurs in " The Child Who Saw Midas " (in the " Troy Park " volume) and in " The Sleeping Beauty ". And many other themes are treated in the same repetitive way ; so that not only a certain diction, but also a certain choice of subject comes to be expected. Yet such is the force of Miss Sitwell's poetic talent that we welcome the convention ; she compels us to believe in her " hen-cackling " grass, her " giggling " fruits, her " clucking " flowers. Less easily accepted are the withdrawals into private recollections. Her " Emily-coloured " primulas and her " Martha-coloured " scabious have a meaning for her [1] which is not communicated to the reader ; and much obscurity in her

---

[1] Presumably ; otherwise it would be peculiarly perverse of Miss Sitwell to quarrel, as she does, with the *surréalistes*, and to complain of André Breton's phrase " cat-headed dew " (" Arthur Rimbaud—an Essay ", *op. cit.*, p. 44).

work is due, not to pattern-making, not to experiment, not even to caprice, but to unwillingness to emerge from the fastnesses of memory. This must be counted a weakness, since a writer is of necessity judged by what he communicates. Yet in a way the weakness is a strength, for her inability to free herself from Troy Park and the family circle has given her a theme on which she can play innumerable and subtle variations. Understanding of the child's view of the world is rarely accompanied by the capacity to transmute such promising material to poetry ; as a rule the reader is fobbed off with the sentimental tarradiddles of a Francis Thompson or a Stevenson. Miss Sitwell has retained a child's romantic imagination while acquiring an adult's power of voluptuous expression. The Cassandra of the family, she raves against the forces which threaten Troy Park ; but even when that Ilion has been destroyed she can recreate it for us. There emerges from her poetry a picture of a life at once remote and familiar : remote, because the reader has left it irrevocably behind him ; familiar, because it was once his own. The picture glitters with a hundred colours foreign to the original, since the poet has enriched it from an experience out of the reach of childhood. She has not merely recreated, she has created a world.

But the Troy Park world is only one of many which her imagination creates. Her greatest achievement is this transformation of the everyday into the stuff of fantasy ; her poetry is a perpetual challenge to reality. And gradually the reader sees that while Miss Sitwell

133

is busy destroying one kind of romanticism she is inventing another. She brings to its invention richness of imagery, an impressive rhetoric, a brilliant technique. She brings the indignation which is the romantic's reaction to a world he is trying to escape. And in the end she does escape. She takes refuge, I have said, in Troy Park. But she finds a still more distant sanctuary. In her verse the discords which torment her as a person suffer metamorphosis ; they become poetry. And so for once we really are confronted with the romantic poetry of escape.

SIEGFRIED SASSOON

SIEGFRIED SASSOON

A serious poet writing in England during the War can
scarcely have failed to be affected by such a cataclysm.
The three poets whom I have discussed were all beginning to publish verse at about the same time : Lawrence's first book of poetry appeared in 1913, Mr.
Eliot's in 1917, Miss Sitwell's in 1915 ; and there is in
the work of each some kind of a reaction to the crisis
through which Europe was passing. Lawrence wrote
war poems, though he was never a soldier ; Miss Sitwell produced occasional poems from the point of view
of the non-combatant ; Mr. Eliot never directly men-
tions the War, but he shares with the other two his
horror of the moral and intellectual disintegration which
was its concomitant. All three are critics of a society
and a civilization which, though they cannot be called
the product of the War, have at least been profoundly
modified by it.

But however violently a non-combatant may have
reacted to the War he cannot have been affected in the
same way as a soldier. In this essay I shall deal with
a War poet proper ; with a writer whose indignation

has been for a time concentrated on the crime of which he was a victim instead of being diffused over its results, and who, having survived the War, illustrates both the reactions and the struggle for recovery of an impressionable mind. Mr. Sassoon's development as a poet is particularly interesting, since his verse falls into three chronological periods ; before, during and after the War. For the first two periods we have as well the evidence of prose autobiography ; in all there is a fairly complete record of response to the emergencies of both war and peace. Here I am concerned principally with his poetry ; I shall refer to the prose only as it amplifies or explains the verse.

Mr. Sassoon's first book, " The Old Huntsman ", was published in 1917—the year of Mr. Eliot's " Prufrock " ; it contains verse written before the War and in two moods during the War ; the early " happy warrior " mood ; the later mood of indignation and disgust. The pre-War verse includes poems written as early as 1908, when he was 22 ; its subjects are of the descriptive and meditative type normal to a young " solitary-minded " poet. " Before Day ", " Morning-Land ", " Dryads ", " An Old French Poet "—the titles are sufficiently indicative of the character of the early work. Throughout this first book the poems not directly concerned with the War are almost all traditional in form and conventional in subject. Mr. Sassoon paints in careful chiaroscuro a landscape under storm and sunlight, or evokes the " shrill-voiced " birds, the " bosky screen " and " cage of golden gloom " of a

" dream-forest ". He writes schoolgirl couplets to the birds and the breeze :

Leave not your bough, my slender song-bird sweet,
But pipe me now your roundelay complete.

Come, gentle breeze, and tarrying on your way,
Whisper my trees what you have seen today ;

he shows us an old broken huntsman looking back on his life, or describes daybreak in a garden with cocks crowing, the lark singing and the lawn still silver-grey. There is nothing individual in the forms except an occasional experiment in the yoking of rhyme and assonance ; the diction is conventionally " poetic " and admits such clichés and archaisms as " roundelay ", " gentle breeze ", " full sweet and fair ". The only distinguishing feature of the early verse is its feeling for English landscape. It is full of intimate pictures of country life : " fieldward boys " at dawn scaring the birds from the orchards ; red-faced maids " clattering about the dairy floor " ; a young huntsman riding " along the yellowing coverts " on a misty September morning. And the poet's mind persistently returns to the images of daybreak and " garden nights " and the sudden blossoming of spring ; to the " green, sun-glinted thicket ", " the golden-windowed morn ", the poplar casting its long shadow on the moonlit grass, and the farm cocks crowing " when hooded night was going ". Even this, of course, is not peculiar to Mr. Sassoon ; " Nature-in-her-Moods ", as Mr. Osbert Sitwell calls it, was a favourite theme of the Georgian poets. Only when he expresses his consciousness of solitude in the midst of his landscapes is there any suggestion of individuality—his consciousness of a loneliness enforced from within :

> For I am alone, a dweller among men
> Hungered for what my heart shall never say.

The solitary habit of mind is emphasized in " Memoirs of a Fox-Hunting Man " (1928), the first volume of the autobiography, which records the experiences of a sensitive young man in a pleasing alien society. The book bears out the evidence of the verse in other ways. It shows the young man living in a summer whose memory afterwards " returns like a bee that comes buzzing into a quiet room where the curtains are drawn on a blazing hot afternoon ". It shows him acutely alive to the sensuous pleasures of hunting, to the early morning start and " the indefinable feeling produced by the yellow candle light and the wintry smelling air from the misty garden ", to the freshness of the " sheep-cropped uplands " and the view back to the low country " with its cock-crowing farms and mist-coiled waterways ". All the feeling for English landscape is here ; all the feeling for that self-sufficient country life which the War was to destroy. The young man is less remarkable for his literary tastes than for his desire to be at ease in the hunting-field—and, one might add, for his ability to enjoy such sports as cubbing. In neither autobiography nor early verse do we detect an independent mind.

When the War came to interrupt his enjoyment of the pursuits of poetry and hunting Mr. Sassoon's first reactions were conventional. The conflagration was, he felt, " inevitable " and " justifiable " ; at the beginning of 1916, soon after his arrival in France, he had not, he tells us, " begun to question the rights and wrongs of the War ". Patriotism was reinforced by a kind of exaltation ; " we are the happy legion," he writes :

> War is our scourge ; yet war has made us wise,
> And fighting for our freedom, we are free.

The defenders of France had their present reward :

> And they are fortunate who fight
> For gleaming landscapes swept and shafted
> And crowned by cloud pavilions white ;
> Hearing such harmonies as might
> Only from Heaven be downward wafted—
> Visions of victory and delight.

And responsibility towards the dead had not yet become a cause of bitterness :

> . . . in the gloom I see your laurell'd head,
> And through your victory I shall win the light.

He even had his occasional moments of militarism :

> To these I turn, in these I trust,
> Brother Lead and Sister Steel.

(Mr. Graves says that " The Kiss " (1916), from which these lines are taken, was originally meant seriously and later offered as a satire.) But it was obvious that this " solitary-minded " young man, who in peace had been hearing Kreisler and reading Johnson and Pope,[1] would soon cease to consider himself fortunate in fighting. All very well for him to take refuge in aloofness :

> I keep such music in my brain
> No din this side of death can quell,—
> Glory exulting over pain,
> And beauty, garlanded in hell.

Gradually the War asserts itself and the " secret music " is drowned :

> O music through my clay,
> When will you sound again ?

He begins to observe, to ask questions. He is forced out of his solitude into a feeling of fellowship with those who, like himself, are called upon to endure the vicissitudes of war. The death of a friend acquaints him with the desire for revenge, and in reaction his belief in the Englishman's right to kill Germans is shaken. He finds himself at last unable to write conventional " poetic " verse about freedom and victory. He has the alternative of refraining from writing war poetry. This he rejects, choosing the difficult alternative of making poetry out of the new truth he is learning.

His transition from the " happy warrior " mood to

[1] " Memoirs of a Fox-Hunting Man ", pp. 110, 148 (Faber & Faber).

the mood of bitter pacifism is clear enough in " The Old Huntsman ". We see his rejection of romantic phrases and ideas :

> Rapture and pale Enchantment and Romance,
> And many a sickly slender lord who'd filled
> My soul long since with lutanies of sin,
> Went home, because they couldn't stand the din,

and his adoption of realistic themes and diction in their place. He no longer writes of the laurelled dead ; instead he writes of the unheroic living. A private writing home to his girl :

> To-night he's in the pink ; but soon he'll die.
> And still the war goes on ; *he* don't know why.

—a man killed while piling bags along the parapet :

> He was a young man with a meagre wife
> And two pale children in a Midland town ;
> He showed the photograph to all his mates ;
> And they considered him a decent chap
> Who did his work and hadn't much to say,
> And always laughed at other people's jokes
> Because he hadn't any of his own.

—a soldier lugging planks down a muddy trench :

> I say that he was Christ ; stiff in the glare,
> And leaning forward from his burdening task,
> Both arms supporting it ; his eyes on mine
> Stared from the woeful head that seemed a mask
> Of mortal pain in Hell's unholy shrine.

—these are the new figures in his landscape. Exaltation turns to an angry cynicism :

> O Jesus, send me a wound today,
> And I'll believe in Your bread and wine,
> And get my bloody old sins washed white !

and pity for the inarticulate soldier has its counterpart in rage against the shirker and the profiteer. He paints a different kind of landscape now :

> The sentry keeps his watch where no one stirs
> But the brown rats, the nimble scavengers.

And even his English landscapes have an ironical twist when seen through the eyes of a stretcher-case :

> There shone the blue serene, the prosperous land,
> Trees, cows and hedges ; skipping these, he scanned
> Large, friendly names that change not with the year,
> Lung Tonic, Mustard, Liver Pills and Beer.

But it is not until " Counter-Attack " (1918) that the ultimate bitterness is reached. In " The Old Huntsman " the memory of his dead friend can still give him a sense of freedom from his circumstances ; he can still, strangely enough, feel " war's a joke " while " dreams are true ". In " Counter-Attack " that freedom has become unattainable. There is no escape from the landscape of death, a landscape where " the stale despair of night " yields to a dawn breaking

> . . . like a face with blinking eyes,
> Pallid, unshaved and thirsty, blind with smoke.

—where the mind is imprisoned within

Sad, smoking, flat horizons, reeking woods,
And foundered trench-lines volleying doom for doom.

—a landscape full of monstrous pitiful figures :

        . . . clumsily bowed
With bombs and guns and shovels and battle-gear,
Men jostle and climb to meet the bristling fire.
Lines of grey, muttering faces, masked with fear,
They leave their trenches, going over the top,
While time ticks blank and busy on their wrists,
And hope, with furtive eyes and grappling fists,
Flounders in mud.

There is no escape from it ; but its prisoners have a duty towards each other, the articulate towards the inarticulate, the conscious towards the drugged. Like Wilfred Owen, Mr. Sassoon felt himself responsible to the victims of the crime of war ; he felt himself called upon to speak for them, to translate their sufferings into poetry which should awaken the conscience of the non-combatant. "All squalid, abject, and inglorious elements in war should be remembered," he wrote in his autobiography ; "Counter-Attack" is for the most part an attempt to record the depths of infamy and terror into which decent unprotesting men were forced from 1914 to 1918. The repulsive details of trench fighting are emphasized—the relics of a rearguard action, the agony of attack and retreat, the eternal presence of death :

The place was rotten with death ; green clumsy legs
High-booted, sprawled and grovelled along the saps ;
And trunks, face downward, in the sucking mud,
Wallowed like trodden sand-bags loosely filled ;

and a savage irony repeats :

> Who'll buy my nice fresh corpses, two a penny ?

He mocks the newspaper stories of trench tours, the traditional pictures of a soldier's end, the futile consolations offered to the survivors of battle, and opposes to them the hideous facts of panic and massacre. Then he turns to the callousness and stupidity which he believes to rule the civilian ; he describes an old man, " gross, goggle-eyed, and full of chat " bragging at the club about his son

> . . . getting all the fun
> At Arras with his nine-inch gun.

—and satirizes the jingoism of politicians and the vicious heroics of the Yellow Press. The War, he feels, is a crime of such magnitude that all other preoccupations are inexcusable ; until it has been expiated we have no right to joy and security :

> What means this metal in windy belfries hung
> When guns are all our need ?

he asks, and with bitter irony concludes :

> Bells are like fierce-browed prelates who proclaim
>   That " if our Lord returned He'd fight for *us* ".
> So let our bells and bishops do the same,
>   Shoulder to shoulder with the motor-bus.

But instead of a world engaged in prayer and fasting he sees complacency and greed ; age smugly accepting the sacrifice of youth, authority with perfunctory con-

dolences speeding " glum heroes up the line to death ".
It is a scene of ugliness unrelieved save in its most
improbable section—the fighting line. In the fighting
line Mr. Sassoon discovers all the virtues which are
lacking elsewhere ; it is here that patience, courage,
endurance and freedom from cant and hatred appear.
There is thus a double contrast in his record of war :
contrast between the soldier and the non-combatant ;
between the soldier and his environment. And loyalty
to the soldier supplies his war-poetry with the positive,
constructive theme which balances its satirical and
destructive qualities. Loyalty torments him equally
whether he is with the troops or away from them.
Absence from the line seems to him a betrayal of dead
and living (" your brothers through our blood ").
This sense of responsibility it is which ultimately defeats
his desire for martyrdom as a conscientious objector :

> . . . Love drove me to rebel.
> Love drives me back to grope with them through hell ;
> And in their tortured eyes I stand forgiven.

And in France he has a more terrible responsibility :

> . . . Can they guess
> The secret burden that is always mine ?—
> Pride in their courage ; pity for their distress ;
> And burning bitterness
> That I must take them to the accursèd Line.

It is a responsibility towards men " mocked by hopeless
longing to regain "

> Bank-holidays, and picture shows, and spats
> And going to the office in the train.—

once more the ironic twist. Something in this simplicity, this desire for the small securities of peace, is intolerably affecting to him ; joined with the unpretentious heroism of the doomed, it moves him to his most consistent and most enduring poetry.

In 1919 Mr. Sassoon published two books of verse : " War Poems ", comprising a selection from " The Old Huntsman " and " Counter-Attack " and twelve new pieces ; and " Picture Show ", a volume privately printed which continued the indictment of war and carried the record of impressions into the beginning of peace, ending with the famous explosion of joy and relief, " Everyone suddenly burst out singing ". The war poems repeat the themes of " Counter-Attack "— compassion and indignation for the butchery of youth and the exploitation of simple obedience ; though two poems have a new setting—Egypt and the returning troopship ; and there is a variation on the sacrifice motive in " Devotion to Duty " with its ironic version of the Bathsheba story. In the verse which is not concerned with the War he appears at a first glance to be slipping back with unexpected ease into pre-war habits of thought. There is a group of love poems set against the background of the " rain-soaked garden " and " the stately gleam of foliage " and daybreak with

> . . . stir of wings ;
> And down the wood a thrush that wakes and sings.

A butterfly provokes the inevitable comparison with the

148

soul in " the phantom glare of day " ; the beauty of transient things enchants him :

Winds, birds, and glittering leaves that flare and fall—

But the return to peace was not as easy as all that ; certainly not for a man who had suffered as much from war as Mr. Sassoon :

> O starshine on the fields of long-ago,
> Bring me the darkness and the nightingale ;
> Dim wealds of vanished summer, peace of home,
> And silence : and the faces of my friends.

Death, for him, always " gropes on the shutter'd pane " ; memory will not let him be. Love itself is disturbed by

> The gloomy stricken places in my soul,
> And the occasional ghosts that haunt my gaze.

Times have changed, and he with them ; even the temple of sport has been deconsecrated. He still writes about his " bird-sung gardens ", it is true, but with a sardonic grimace ; and he threatens one day to astonish his admirers with " a dark tremendous song " not at all to their taste. Always at the back of his mind is the old feeling of loyalty to the dead : the dead who must not be forgotten lest the crime of war should be repeated.

It was over six years before he again published a book of verse, " Satirical Poems " (1926). In the meantime he had been watching Europe's return to peace and finding it disappointing ; this disappointment is the theme of the new book. His verse is now and then switched back to the War by some ironical turn of events ; by the publication of a diplomat's war diary :

> The visionless officialized fatuity
> That once kept Europe safe for Perpetuity.

—by the presence at a Founder's Feast of " great Major-General Bluff ". But for the most part it is concentrated on the preoccupations of a world newly at peace. He satirizes the fatuous pomp of the Wembley exhibition ; the vulgarity of the popular press ; the materialism of New York ; the vacant ostentation of the theatre and the snobbery of its audiences. Is this, he asks himself, the reaction of a civilized world to its escape from annihilation ? Everywhere he sees the trivial response to the profound appeal, whether it is made in the concert hall or in the drawing-room ; everywhere he sees wealth misused and taste degraded. And, remembering the virtues of his companions in the War, men from a class rarely encountered in concert hall or drawing-room, he revolts against his own class. In 1919 Mr. Sassoon was literary editor of the " Daily Herald " ; and throughout the " Satirical Poems " he proclaims his socialistic principles. He puts " the case for the miners " ; satirizes the hotel *de luxe* and its visitors " poisoned by possession " ; moralizes on the demolition of Devonshire House ; ridicules a snobbish Society and an obsolete aristocracy. And with his adoption of socialism many changes appear in his

views. I have already hinted at his declining interest
in sport ; now we see him

> Grow half-humane, and question the propriety
> Of *Foxes Torn to Bits in Smart Society*.

And, since the humanitarian and the social reformer
are apt to despise the scholar and the historian, we find
him joining in the popular prejudices against museums
and the study of the past ; we find him making the
facile vulgar contrast between life and art, and dis-
covering romance not in Turner but in his copyist :

> . . . Now my heart
> Leaps towards Romance and knows it, standing there
> In that calm student with the red-brown hair,
> Copying *The Death of Chatterton* with care
> And missing all the magic. That young head
> Is life, the unending challenge. . . . Turner's dead.

But in his search for victims he does not spare himself ;
his new satirical style laughs at his earlier, derivative,
" poetic " style, at his " pursuance of the encharioted
Sublime ", at the professional mood in which he visits
the ready-made romantic scene of the Villa d'Este
gardens :

> Those fountains, too, " like ghosts of cypresses " ;—
> (The phrase occurred to me while I was leaning
> On an old balustrade ; imbibing sunset ;
> Wrapped in my verse vocation)—how they linked me
> With Byron, Landor, Liszt, and Robert Browning ! . . .

I say advisedly his " search for victims " ; for his
bitterness against the post-war world is not content

with the legitimate objects of satire ; it turns its heavy
artillery on such targets as a middle-aged Dean whose
only crime seems to be regular attendance at the
'Varsity cricket match. Even when he is not writing
about the War, Mr. Sassoon is still possessed by the
bitterness it engendered.

He was to make an effort to rid himself of his nightmare. In 1928, the year in which the first volume of
the autobiography appeared, " The Heart's Journey "
was published. The opening invocation shows at once
that he is trying to retrace his steps :

> Soul, be my song ; return arrayed in white ;
> Lead home the loves that I have wronged and slain ;
> Bring back the summer dawns that banished night
> With distant-warbling bird-notes after rain . . .
> Time's way-worn traveller I. And you, O song,
> O soul, my Paradise laid waste so long.

He is returning, astonishingly enough, to " familiar
fields and star-tossed trees ", to the " leaf-shadow-
latticed grass " and the early sunlight " shadowless with
misty gold " ; he has heard the annunciation of an
" ultimate Spring ". He has not put the War out of
his mind ; the Menin Gate is still to him a " sepulchre
of crime ". But he seems to have escaped from the
shadow of war. Faith has been absolved from the fear
of annihilation :

> . . . I saw in a dream the dead
> Moving among green trees.
> I saw the living green
> Uprising from the rock.

And he proclaims his belief in the immortality of thought. It is as if he were setting himself to answer the challenge of his satirical work. We hear no more of the living copyist and the dead original ; it is from the work of an eighteenth-century writer that he learns how poetry " plays tricks with death ", and once more he turns to the " dead musicians " whom as a soldier he rejected. Solitude once more awaits him in " contemplative candleshine ". For the moment declaring a truce with society, he recalls the spell of " latening twilight sure with spring ", and adds to the old simplicity of sense a new simplicity of mind, " the peace that shines apart ".

> O flower within me wondrous white,
> I know you only as my need
> And my unsealed sight.

It is the rediscovery of peace. But it is also a return to dilettantism ; the honesty which informs the war poetry has been succeeded by a readiness to make shift with the poet's stock-in-trade. The post-war verse has no certain anchorage ; and these meditative pieces are not free of the general insecurity. In 1933 a group of six satirical poems, " The Road to Ruin ", showed that Mr. Sassoon was still living on the memory of anger.[1] The theme is the war to come, the war of bacterial bombs and poison gas for civilians :

---

[1] Before this Mr. Sassoon, under the pseudonym " Pinchbeck Lyre ", had produced a group of brilliant parodies of Mr. Humbert Wolfe's poetry.

" We honour here " (he paused) " our Million Dead ;
Who, as a living poet has nobly said,
' Are now forever London.'   Our bequest
Is to rebuild, for What-they-died-for's sake,
A bomb-proof roofed Metropolis, and to make
Gas-drill compulsory.   *Dulce et decorum est . . .*"

But it is the last war of which he is thinking ; fifteen
years after the Armistice he is looking, not forward, but
back.

.   .   .   .

I have pointed out that the language of the early
verse was smooth, conventional and full of clichés.
And I have said that with the change in his ideas about
war comes a change in his poetic diction ; that romantic
phrases are discarded for realistic descriptions, heroics
for satire.   It is, indeed, a violent reversal.   Instead of
the shrill-voiced birds in their " cage of golden gloom "
he hears the rumour of battle :

> . . . sometimes a bullet sang,
> And droning shells burst with a hollow bang ;

instead of " cloud pavilions white " he sees a livid
horizon :

> . . . Ghastly dawn with vaporous coasts
> Gleams desolate along the sky, night's misery ended.

The " roundelay " of spring is drowned in " a blurred
confusion of yells and groans ".   The happy legion is
transformed into a company of

> . . . dazed, muttering creatures underground
> Who hear the boom of shells in muffled sound.

And the army of the dead, " dawn-lit trees " hailing
" the burning heavens they left unsung ", dwindles to
a charnel-heap of

> . . . naked sodden buttocks, mats of hair,
> Bulged clotted heads . . .

Always the violent phrase, the grating epithet ; romantic clichés are ousted by colloquialisms and slang, and
smooth cadences by the jerky motions of anger. He
does not abandon traditional forms : blank verse, the
sonnet and the rhymed stanza are the vehicle for his
bitterest indictments of war. But within those forms all
the romantic conventions are flouted :

> When Dick was killed last week he looked like that,
> Flapping along the fire-step like a fish,
>
> " The war'll be over soon."
> > " What 'opes ? "
> > " No bloody fear ! "
>
> Do you remember the rats ; and the stench
> Of corpses rotting in front of the front-line trench,—

the images are uncouth, the diction is rough ; and the
sound of the verse is deliberately harsh :

> He winked his prying torch with patching glare

Mr. Sassoon makes play with staccato alliteration and
the impact of warring consonants, or by the use of
heavy droning vowels he deepens the impression of
immitigable gloom. The identification of mood and
manner is almost complete.

When we come to the satirical poems we find a further coarsening of technique. Alliteration has been carried to its limits. Mr. Sassoon goes to Wembley and sees " patriotic paradings with pygmy preciseness " ; to Wittelsbach, and notes how " drab drugget paths protect these polished floors " ; to the rooms of a prehistorian, and listens while

> An archaeologist began to make
> Assumptions about aqueducts

to the Academy, and finds himself " pledged to practise cogitant concision ". But it is not the fastidious alliteration of an artist. His words echo one another with savage redundance ; it is the virtuosity of a writer whose moral preoccupations have made him despise his own technique. The talents which in the war poetry were used for realistic description are now turned to the fabrication of baroque phrases ; the verse loses its look of direct truth and becomes self-consciously ornate. Mendelssohn is the musician of " Love's macassar-oiled Magnificat " ; the " faded pink façade " of Scutcheon Hall is a

> . . . nectarine
> Of pre-taxation Rent-roll style-stability
> Planned for an impermutable nobility.

The Villa d'Este gardens are " spired with pinaceous ornamental gloom ". Stravinsky's " Sacré du Printemps " is preluded by

> . . . vibro-atmospheric copulations
> With mezzo-forte mysteries of noise

The weight of the adjectives grows oppressive : as oppressive as the bitter sophistication of the verse in general. And the technique with its air of bravado emphasizes Mr. Sassoon's contempt for the objects of his satire. It is a contempt which embraces not only the " cultural inferno " of the Sunday performance stalls, not only the " unspeculative faces " of the mob and the " evening-party eyes " of the sempiternal hostess, but also, as I have said, himself. Freed from the demands of war, he has time for introspection ; and his peevish inward gaze sees a professional in words, a man with a note-book, " Clothed in the gilded surname of Sassoon ".

With " The Heart's Journey " comes a reaction. The arrogant ornateness of the satires has vanished ; in its place is a studied simplicity. The diction once again becomes smooth and romantic : " the cloisters of my heart " ; " Those tired sweet drowsy words we left unsaid " ; " flocks of silver angels " ; " Drifts of blossoms flushed and fell ". Mr. Sassoon makes use of such poetic properties as stars, trees and flowers ; the words " Paradise " and " Elysian " are repeated ; patience and stillness are now the subjects of his verse, and the Muse, once the butt of a half-contemptuous cynicism, is again treated with old-fashioned courtesy. But with technique as well as with theme there is a kind of vacillation, an inability to move steadily in one direction ; and " The Road to Ruin ", returning to the subjects, returns also in some measure to the manner of the " Satirical Poems "—to their alliteration and heavy decoration. In both reflective and satirical verses certainty of line is wanting. Lack of a contemporary anchorage drives him back to the past ; and a failure of confidence even in poetry forces his style to turn in upon itself, to take refuge from the truth of art in the easy and the familiar.

.   .   .   .   .   .

Mr. Sassoon represents a generation of young writers who were snatched from the preoccupations of peace and suddenly faced with the immense facts of pain and death. Some would without this stimulus have turned to the writing of realistic or revolutionary verse ; Mr. Sassoon was not, I think, among them. His early poetry is sometimes talented but never original ; without the War he might never have become more than a writer of moderate Georgian verse. The War did two things for him as a poet. It confronted him with realities to which in peace he had been indifferent ; and while providing the stimulus to write seriously, it also provided material which was in itself immensely important. He rose to his opportunities ; the better for his early habits of mind. I have spoken of his feeling for English landscape ; the feeling was to intensify the horror of the landscapes of war, while they in their turn were to throw into relief the quiet and the security of England. He is haunted by the softer aspects of the country-side : by the " rain-washed skies " and the " rain-soaked garden " ; the " dew-soaked lawn " and the " dripping summer garden " are a recurring motive in his prose ; and amidst agonizing recollections of war it is for a thunderstorm he wishes,

> With bucketsful of water to sluice the dark
> And make the roses hang their dripping heads.

This passion for a " life-learned landscape " supplies much of the contrast in his war poems, and from time to time illumines even the fields of death. The effect of his denunciation is far greater for the background of remembered peace, " the land of lost content ".

The second quality of his early verse, its consciousness of solitude, seems at first to be lost in the war period ; it is replaced by a sense of responsibility for those less articulate than himself. Then it reappears in a curious form. He no longer feels, it is true, that he is living apart from the world of men ; but he begins to feel that, together with his fellow-victims, he is cut off from every world except that of war.

> Soldiers are citizens of death's gray land,

they are no longer concerned with the business of life. He begins to think of himself as a member of a doomed society.[1] Outside that society the civilian carries on the ordinary pursuits of peace ; but the soldier is no longer able to feel that the pursuits of peace have any reality, and the non-combatant assumes for him the qualities of " callousness " and " complacency ". When

[1] Cf. the consciousness of isolation in the work of Mr. Auden and Mr. Day Lewis.

he comes to write his autobiography he confesses to an occasional doubt about the " callous complacency " of those at home. But at the time of writing the war verse he has, apparently, no doubt ; the result is an output of sustained bitterness, a poetic record of a terrible single-mindedness.

I do not think that his war poetry loses anything by being one-sided. His rôle is that of the accuser ; he plays it the better for his emphasis on the " squalid, abject and inglorious ". It is when we come to the post-war verse that one-sidedness becomes a fault. The War gave him a magnificent theme for satire ; passing, it left him with a residue of anger for which there was no sufficient object. He is like Hamlet in Mr. Eliot's analysis, a man baffled by " the absence of objective equivalent to his feelings ".[1] His world has been turned upside down by the massacre from which he has escaped ; seeking an outlet for his discontent, he expends his scorn upon trivial unoffending objects. The later satires are valuable as an expression of post-war psychology, but the discrepancy between subject and treatment invalidates them as poetry.

The parallels between the prose and the verse are significant. Like Lawrence, like Miss Sitwell, Mr. Sassoon often treats the same theme in prose and in verse, and uses in both the same phrases, the same set of images. The " livid face of a dead German whose fingers still clutched the blackened gash on his neck "[2]

[1] " The Sacred Wood ", p. 101.
[2] " Memoirs of an Infantry Officer ", p. 225 (Faber & Faber).

of " Memoirs of an Infantry Officer " is repeated in the

> . . . livid face
> Terribly glaring up, whose eyes yet wore
> Agony dying hard ten days before ;
> And fists of fingers clutched a blackening wound.—

of " The Rear-Guard ". The poem " Died of Wounds "
is reproduced almost word for word in the prose.[1]
The " blurred orange sunset ", the thistle-tufts and
mouth-organs and " murmur of voices, gruff, confused
and low " of " At Carnoy " are all to be found in the
prose description of a concentration point near Mametz.[2]
Here is a passage from " Memoirs of a Fox-Hunting
Man " : " Candles and braziers glinted through the
curtain-flaps and voices muttered gruffly from the little
underground cabins. Now and again there was the
splitting crack of a rifle-shot from the other side, or a
five-nine shell droned serenely across the upper air to
burst with a hollow bang. . . . The shallow blanching
flare of a rocket gave me a glimpse of the mounds of
bleached sandbags on the Redoubt. Its brief whiteness
died downward, leaving a dark world ; chilly gusts met
me at corners, piping drearily through crannies of the
parapet ".[3] And here is the version of " A Working
Party " :

> Candles and braziers glinted through the chinks
> And curtain-flaps of dug-outs ; then the gloom
> Swallowed his sense of sight ; he stooped and swore
> Because a sagging wire had caught his neck.

---

[1] Ibid., p. 123.   [2] Ibid., p. 80.   [3] p. 380.

A flare went up ; the shining whiteness spread
And flickered upward, showing nimble rats,
And mounds of glimmering sand-bags, bleached with rain
Then the slow, silver moment died in dark.

The wind came posting by with chilly gusts
And buffeting at corners, piping thin
And dreary through the crannies ; rifle-shots
Would split and crack and sing along the night,
And shells came calmly through the drizzling air
To burst with hollow bank below the hill.

Again and again the phrases are identical ; the prose merely uses them more smoothly than the verse. The verse, it is true, often adds a fine descriptive touch : " Then the slow, silver moment died in dark " ; more often the demands of metre give it an artificial quality absent from the prose. As far as descriptive writing is concerned, in fact, these parallel passages show him as better at his ease in prose than in verse ; and in general the prose autobiography is a more complete and unaffected record of experience than the poetry. Individual poems are sometimes richer than anything in the Prose : for instance, the noble tranquil "Death-Bed" (1916). And there are phrases in the verse with an intensity and a sharpness which the autobiography never achieves :

. . . the instant split
His startled life with lead, and all went out.

. . . time ticks blank and busy on their wrists,

He climbed through darkness to the twilight air,
Unloading hell behind him step by step.

But they are nearly always phrases inspired by the terror and cruelty of war ; it becomes steadily more obvious that Mr. Sassoon's greatest talent in verse is for denunciation. And so we come back to the question of the poet's material—and find the accuser indebted for his success to the magnitude of the crime he denounces. The subject transcends its treatment : Mr. Sassoon's war poetry is greater than Mr. Sassoon's talent. The prose has grace and warmth for which we look in vain in the verse. But there is in the verse a piercing anger for which the prose is never an adequate vehicle. We see in " The Old Huntsman " and " Counter-Attack " and " Picture Show " the despair, the helpless indignation of a doomed and guiltless generation. It is the soldier's point of view, but it is more than that ; the War possessed Mr. Sassoon and used him as an instrument for its accusation. In this expression of a calamity greater even than his own conception of it lies the lasting importance of his poetry.

Technically he has had no direct influence ; though undoubtedly his war poetry has helped to break down a tradition : the tradition of temperate sentiment and well-bred expression which is past saving in the work of Laurence Binyon. After the honesty of " Counter-Attack ", conventional substitutes for poetry began to appear less plausible. But Mr. Sassoon's talent, we have seen, was not strong enough to carry him into the future and there to shape the forms of poetry according to its own need. Contemporaneity is not in itself a merit. For once, however, its apostles have some slight justification. One of the weaknesses of his later work is that it shirks the present. Miss Sitwell, too, is a fugitive from the present. But hers is, as I have said, not merely an evasion into the past ; it is by accepting the challenge of poetry that she escapes. Mr. Sassoon's poetry is not powerful enough to sustain him in resisting a destructive experience. For a short period that experience was put to the uses of poetry ; then it gained the upper hand ; now it holds him a prisoner in the past. Like many of his generation, he continued to live in a state of war long after peace had been signed. It might have done his poetry no harm had he brought fresh experience to bear on the old themes. This he never did ; here, and not in any choice of subject, is the failure in contemporaneity.

The war poetry was a contemporary record of the impressions of a mind clinging to sanity in a mad world ; the post-war verse shows us that mind in some way defeated by its conflict. Psychologically, in his lack of orientation since 1918, Mr. Sassoon is representative of a great number of his generation. But his work has a further historical significance. For it is against such an attitude as his that the new generation of poets rebel. Where he looks back they look forward ; where he suffers, they preach a cure ; where he indicts the heritage of the past, they proclaim a revolution. His reactions have thus been instrumental in opening a way for a new movement. But ultimately it is for his contribution to the literature of the war period that he must be judged. And in that he must be recognized as a man called on to denounce a sacrifice, and made equal to his task by the strength of his indignation.

ADVANCE GUARD

ADVANCE GUARD

The writers discussed in the foregoing essays unite in one characteristic—aversion from post-war civilization. It is not an accidental relationship. The quality which has most impressed critics of post-war verse has been its disillusion. A generation had grown up lacking a solid moral and intellectual foothold and blaming society for not offering it ; for some years serious poets have been occupied in denying the civilization which produced them. These four writers, Lawrence, Mr. Eliot, Miss Sitwell and Mr. Sassoon, thus seem to me in some measure representative of the main currents of poetry for the last two decades ; in negation at least they are at one.

Obviously their reactions to the civilization in whose midst they are rebels have been sharply different. Lawrence and Mr. Eliot found themselves faced with the same problem ; the reconciliation of an abnormal sensibility with a hostile society. Many poets have found themselves in such a position ; and we need not imagine that in another age the discord would have been necessarily less strident. The peculiarity lies in the fact that for both of them the problem became a moral problem. For Lawrence it was never anything

167

else. He had, it is true, frequent and violent aesthetic reactions : to landscape, flowers, trees, animals—usually in fact to natural phenomena ; more rarely to literature. But whenever possible he turned the aesthetic reaction into a moral judgment (his literary criticism as literary criticism is generally worthless for this reason). Gradually aesthetic sensibility was overlaid by moral sensibility ; the discord thinned to a clash between an austerely moral nature and a decadent social morality ; the problem, never complex, became terrifyingly simple : how to escape from the wrath present and to come. Unhesitatingly his instinct pointed the way. Physical experiences had long seemed to him the most valid ; physical relationships had long seemed the least corrupt. From this it is only a step to conviction that salvation must come through the body. But physical impulses, he felt, were controlled by some irresistible power. Not by the " spirit " ; certainly not by the mind ; Lawrence, clever man though he himself was, rejected as fallacious the claims of the reason. Control comes from the " deepest instincts ", echoes within us of the universal rhythm. The true morality lies in submission to these " deepest instincts ", to the unconscious : in fact to the irrational. We have arrived at the negation not only of Christian " spirituality ", but also of the intellectualism which undermines it ; Lawrence has become an apostle of the new anti-rationalist movement. He would have been horrified to think that he was aligning himself with Freud,[1] the *surréalistes* and Mr. G. K. Chesterton.

[1] But see Thomas Mann's article in " The Criterion ", July, 1933.

168

For Mr. Eliot the problem is complicated by aesthetic and intellectual preoccupations too insistent to be overlaid ; a part-answer to the questions they raise is found in his criticism and in the technique of his verse. The main discord, as with Lawrence, is moral : austerity against indifference, single-mindedness against chaos. But it must be resolved in a different way. There is no help in the physical ; Mr. Eliot begins with a mistrust of the body which deepens as time goes on to enmity. And while Lawrence becomes more certain, not of the perfectibility of man, but of the innate morality of man uncorrupted by self-consciousness, Mr. Eliot becomes more certain of original sin. Submission, if a submission is to be made, clearly must not be to the unconscious.[1] Which way, then, lies escape ? Through the intellect ? Unequal to obliterating the disgust which torments him. Mr. Eliot takes the time-honoured way out : in submission to the authority of Christianity. To many people this would seem an evasion of the problem ; I have tried to show that for him it was the only possible solution. But not an easy solution, as " Ash Wednesday " proves. It implies an intellectual surrender which to such a temperament must have been hardly tolerable ; it implies, indeed, a surrender to the irrational which one might compare with Lawrence's were it not that Lawrence submits instinctively and blindly, Mr. Eliot deliberately and with his eyes open. The difference between the two

[1] For Mr. Eliot, Lawrence's submission is to the Powers of Evil. Cf. " After Strange Gods ".

writers is further defined when the surrender has been made. Lawrence was born and remained an artist—but an artist who prized the gift of prophecy above the gift of art ; once he had seen a solution to his own problem he inevitably preached that solution as a universal gospel. Mr. Eliot is prevented by something beyond dislike of redundancy from becoming a prophet of Christianity. Caring much for art, he cares little for gospel-riding ; having once recognized a harmony —the harmony which Lawrence thought it unworthy to seek—he is content to pursue it for his own necessity —and for the necessity of poetry.

Clearly Mr. Sassoon is at best a minor poet. But historically this makes his point of view the more interesting. It shows us that the lesser as well as the greater sensibility is jarred by modern society ; it proves a degree of unanimity between the most dissimilar minds. We must remember, of course, that his quarrel with society dates from the War ; his problem does not beset him until he has been forced out of his normal course of life. When it did present itself it burst like a moral hurricane into his mild aesthetic preoccupations. The world as he saw it was suddenly split into contradictions : the simple sensuous pleasures of peace, the miseries of war ; the sufferings of the combatant, the indifference of the civilian ; the courage and integrity of the fighting ranks, the incompetence and dishonesty of the politicians. Mr. Sassoon from a dilettante was transformed into a man of wrath. But when peace returned it found him psychologically and

aesthetically disorientated. Up to this point he con-
veniently represents the generation of war poets. Of
these one—Wilfred Owen—showed himself able to fuse
the discordant elements of war into a poetic unity ; he
did not live to see peace. For most of the others the
tension between life and death was too great, the shock
to the sensibilities too prolonged ; when war ended
they had lost sympathy with the old modes of poetry
without acquiring the power to create new ones. Mr.
Sassoon in his post-war satires tried to invent an individual style apt to his new mood of cynicism and disgust.
But the problem of tackling the *whole* of the material,
of admitting to poetry the *whole* series of his impressions,
and creating from the clash between society and his
by now unassuageable sensibilities an inviolable unity
—that problem he evaded. He refused to take what
Lawrence would have called the next step into the
future ; instead, as we have seen, he took a step back.
But even if his development stops there he remains
interesting as a minor sensibility temporarily heightened
to major sensibility : as an example of a writer intended
by nature for temperate responses to gentle stimuli, and
driven by the exigencies of our time into uncontrollable
grief and anger.

At a first glance Miss Sitwell's poetry appears un-
related to that of the foregoing writers. She is, to begin
with, more concerned to escape from moral problems
than to solve them. Her sensibilities are first and fore-
most aesthetic ; but she has, too, a purely personal
problem to solve : how to come to terms—any kind of

terms—with her immediate surroundings. She never does come to terms ; instead she takes refuge, not, like Mr. Sassoon, in dilettantism, but in poetry. Within that refuge she can give play to her aesthetic sensibilities : in experiments with technique, in surrender to dream. For Miss Sitwell, too, submits to the irrational, though her irrationalism is aesthetic and not moral. Still it links her with the movement in which Lawrence, as we have seen, plays a part. Nor can she wholly evade moral issues. Now and then indignation jerks her out of her dream ; treachery stabs her, the callousness of wealth built on misery goads her into invective. Fundamentally her attitude towards postwar civilization resembles that of the three writers previously discussed. Mr. Sassoon is forced by circumstances, Lawrence and Mr. Eliot are driven by moral discord into hostility ; Miss Sitwell from the beginning never resists a profound anti-social instinct.

. . . .

By the end of the twenties a reaction was due, and several young men had decided that disillusion had been worked out. An assurance is suddenly expressed that, as Mr. Leavis puts it, " there is a course to steer, that bearings can be found, that there is a possible readjustment to the conditions ".[1] Or a possible readjustment of the conditions ; for the writers I shall discuss do not attempt to reconcile the poetic sensibility with society ; it is their concern so to reform society that the poet will no longer be in conflict with it. In the ideal state

[1] " New Bearings in English Poetry ", p. 206.

there will be no anti-social poets. Lawrence, too, wanted to reform society ; and the new generation is much influenced by Lawrence. But with him the rejection of the framework of civilization dies down at last to a despairing rejection of civilization itself. The younger generation have no place for despair. " The writers in this book ", says Mr. Michael Roberts in his preface to the anthology, " New Signatures ", "'have learned to accept the fact that progress is illusory, and yet to believe that the game is worth playing ; to believe that the alleviation of suffering is good even though it merely makes possible new sensitiveness and therefore new suffering. . . ." [1] Mr. Roberts is not exact. The writers in his anthology, among them Mr. W. H. Auden, Mr. Cecil Day Lewis, and Mr. Stephen Spender, have *not* learned to accept the fact that progress is illusory. They are even certain of the direction in which progress is possible. Lawrence, though he preached salvation, confused his disciples by the vagueness of his prescriptions. The advance guard prescribe the remedy in which he had least confidence : a political creed.

In 1930 Mr. Auden's first book, " Poems ", was published. It was clear at once that here was a strong and confident talent. Mr. Auden was under no necessity to struggle painfully with the difficulties of Mr. Eliot and Mr. Joyce ; he belonged to the generation to which I have already referred,[2] a generation born to familiarity with the new idioms and self-schooled in their obscurity. When he came to write verse himself he lisped in riddles,

[1] p. 12.   [2] Cf. p. 97.

for the riddles came ; sometimes he lisped in riddles
when a plain statement would have done as well. Nor
was there anything in the post-war doctrines of literature to dismay him ; he had been bred on disillusion.
Now he rejected it. If he gave allegiance it was to
Lawrence, to the single poet of affirmation of the post-
war years. But at best it was a half-allegiance. Mr.
Auden did not find sex a religious subject : nor did he
believe in resurrection.

He begins, however, with negation, with implication
rather than statement. " Paid on Both Sides ", the
" charade " with which " Poems " opens, does not
preach new life : it assails the old death-order which
he believes to be strangling Europe. It shows us the
combatants in an inextinguishable feud trapped and
hopeless of escape : " no news but the new death ".
It is a feud nourished by the familiar clichés : " we
cannot betray the dead "—and whipped on by its own
follies ; despair, " that soon-arriving day ", holds the
fighters bound. Only a break with the past can end
the breeding of wrongs. And that break is never made ;
the idea of vengeance is too strong.

> The hands that were to help will not be lifted,
> And bad followed by worse leaves to us tears,
> An empty bed, hope from less noble men.
> I had seen joy
> Received and given, upon both sides, for years.
> Now not.

Pacifism ; a break with tradition ; rejection of the
practice of an older generation—these are the bases of

Mr. Auden's attack. They emerge more clearly in the poems which form the second part of the book. The ancestral curse, he says, has fallen, the curse of decay which follows arrested evolution. The burden of the past is breaking England—a tradition " wrong for years ". And with despair he points to the slowing down of industry, to abandoned mines and empty factories, silent wharves and idle ships. Like Lawrence, he prophesies disaster. There is a sinister moment of quiet before the crash. But terror draws closer, the glacier creeps down ; paralysis binds the doomed. Soon the mob will break loose.

> You cannot be away, then, no
> Not though you pack to leave within an hour,
> Escaping humming down arterial roads :

The heroes of doomsday can expect little beyond a respectable defeat. But for the honest man there is no choice between inertia and resistance.

> As for ourselves there is left remaining
> Our honour at least,
> And a reasonable chance of retaining
> Our faculties to the last.

Nothing more.

Unless there is " a change of heart ". For, like Lawrence again, this time Mr. Auden exhorts to new life. A new life dependent on " the destruction of error ", on the " death of the old gang " : in short, on discarding the past. This may be pacifism ; but it is militant pacifism. Suddenly we are confronted with

an affirmation : there *is* " a course to steer ". Our
need is for

> . . . a sovereign touch
> Curing the intolerable neural itch,
> The exhaustion of weaning, the liar's quinsy,
> And the distortions of ingrown virginity.
> Prohibit sharply the rehearsed response
> And gradually correct the coward's stance ;
> Cover in time with beams those in retreat
> That, spotted, they turn though the reverse were great ;

It is, one sees, a moral course ; he is preaching, not,
it is true, muscular christianity, but certainly muscular
ethics.

But so far it has not been made clear how we are to
set about curing the distortions of ingrown virginity.
In " The Orators " (1932) prophecy is still stronger
than precept. This " English study ", as Mr. Auden
calls it, contains firstly a group of prose pieces under
the general title " The Initiates ". Here are subtle
warnings against private and civic degeneracy ; a
hinted story of another Messiah betrayed : [1] a Joycean
catalogue of those awaiting deliverance : an allegorical
threat of crisis. Book II, " Journal of an Airman ",
wraps the same themes in denser obscurity. In the
work of the advance guard the aeronaut is always on
the right side : he stands for speed, height, strength,
courage, progress, the future and no nonsense about
individualism ; and this Airman is found struggling,
in a mixture of prose and verse, against both personal

---

[1] It has been suggested that this refers to Lawrence.

weakness and national peril. Stealthily the unnamed Enemy who haunts Mr. Auden's writings pushes forward his outposts. In vain the Airman notes his disguises, his gambits, his catchwords—" insure now—keep smiling—safety first " : his clothing—" fisherman's pockets—Dickens' waistcoats—adhesive trousers " : his occupations—" playing cards—collecting—talking to animals ". Sometimes this Protean adversary is a newspaper proprietor, sometimes an Oxford Don, sometimes just a tedious elderly gentleman ; public inertia persists in face of every mode of attack. The Airman dreams of Lawrentian counter-attack in the manner of " The Plumed Serpent " :

The two dance leaders chosen quietly by lot.
The faggots for the beacon carted this morning
Up the Highwayman's Road, the cases of rockets . . .
We have done as he said ; we have not forgotten his promise.
" Your desire shall be granted when the time is perfect,
Let the moon be a sign to your eyes of the trust,
Assemble all of you when the moon is full,
The power shall fill you, the touch be restored."

The musicians are having their final rehearsal ;
The town seems stiller, our greetings quieter than usual.
O charged-to-the-full-in-secret slow-beating heart,
To-night is full-moon.

But it is too late. Already the final enemy attack is ordered—an Ulysses-like *coup d'état* which, opening with " predictions of defeat made by wireless-controlled crows and card-packs ", advances through " epidemics of lupus, halitosis, and superfluous hair " to the last judgment : " Pressure of ice, falling fire. The last snarl of families beneath the toppling column. Biting at wounds as the sutures tear." And the Airman takes the only way out : suicide.

Lastly six Odes. The same melancholy retrospect over hopeless Europe and England ravaged by Giant Sloths and Giant Despairs. The same picture of decay, material and spiritual :

> Saying Alas
> To less and less.

The same warnings against the Enemy, against the raids of Fear, Lust, Wrath ; the same story of despairing heroism in counter-attack. But of the change of heart more hope. There must, it seems, be a moral renaissance of a violent kind : a renaissance of hardihood and toughness, optimism and noise ; a renaissance in short with the common characteristics of black shirt, brown shirt and red flag. This accomplished, there is still a chance for the slacker and the loafer, for " unhappy Joseph " and " repressed Diana " ; even the " cissy " will go for " cross-country runs ". Morality has become, not merely muscular, but also athletic ; revivalism has joined forces with the public school spirit. It is difficult to believe that only ten years earlier " The Waste Land " was making educated despair fashionable.

We see, then, in the early work a move from despair to a desperate hope : a move from inertia towards a militant morality. There is another characteristic of the first two books : their peculiar obscurity. It is not

the obscurity of an Eliot or a Joyce, not obscurity
produced by erudite allusions or by idiosyncrasies of
language : Mr. Auden in his character as revivalist
despises the surrender to the past implied in a purely
literary virtuosity. It is a difficulty proceeding firstly
from omission. Thought is stripped of its connecting
links ; the verse becomes so athletic that it can scarcely
be followed. The use of spare, almost monosyllabic
diction often lends a deceptive air of candour to the
poems ; this is particularly the case with those treating of personal relationships, of " the heart's changes ",
of " a backward love ", of the move " From yes to no ".
For Mr. Auden's work includes a personal as well as
an impersonal poetry : its difficulty is due in the second
place to the invasion of the impersonal by the personal.
Not only personal, but also private. Already in the
" Poems " there are references to characters and occasions of which the ordinary reader can have no knowledge : in " The Orators " the allusions are often so
particular as to be incomprehensible except to the professional gossip. " Gabriel ", " a lot about the Essay
Club and Stephen ", " an economics Don called
Harrod ", " Dick " who " had returned from Germany
in love "—a verse passage in " Journal of an Airman "
is made up almost entirely of private reminiscences.
We may ascribe the development of this narrowly personal manner partly to intolerance of the traditional
graces of poetry, partly to a belief in the intrinsic virtue
of the group. For despite its individualistic air the
verse is rooted in a feeling of solidarity : solidarity with

that section of Mr. Auden's own generation which shares
his horror at a disintegrating England. But his own
generation are only the pioneers of a new life ; it is
from the growing generation that achievement may be
expected. With the growing generation the poetry
frequently tries to equalize itself : like a schoolmaster
in search of popularity, it talks down to its audience.
Hence the playing-field boisterousness of certain passages
in " The Orators ". One of the Odes is a bastard
Pythian with the return of a victorious school Fifteen
as theme. Neither subject nor treatment is adult : the
Ode, beginning with a running commentary on play :

Over and over again we yelled
" Let the ball out to Sergy ! " They did, he scored, and we
    dance.—

goes on to a newspaper report on the homecoming of
the defeated team :

. . . a hushed school receives them in a drizzle,
Clambering, sodden, from a maundering chara., licked to the
    wide.—

and ends with the sickening moral reflections on work
and play which have been familiar since Speech Days
became news. But not only the animal spirits of a foot-
ball team delight Mr. Auden : he is delighted, too, by
its unity of action. He is moving towards the idea of
communism. But it threatens to be communism of a
very public school type.

    A group of verses published in the anthology " New
Country " (1933) shows how far he has moved. " A

Communist to Others " is both a declaration of faith and a challenge to other creeds : the creed of the country-house ruling classes : of the mystic : of the economist : of the psychologist ; and the poem ends with an appeal to poetry to renounce its isolation and return to human tenderness, and with an assurance to the proletariat of indissoluble brotherhood :

> Remember that in each direction
> Love outside our own election
> Holds us in unseen connection :
> O trust that ever.

Here at last the idea of communism emerges clearly. But in the other poems it is only vaguely enunciated. It is a dream of a Lawrentian new life which possesses him ; or else, looking on the

> . . . blurring images
> Of the dingy difficult life of our generation.—

he hopes only for sanity in the growing generation. The long satirical piece " A Happy New Year " shows that he has learned more from Lawrence than contempt for a shoddy civilization. The " Lords of limit ", the " influential quiet twins " he invokes are the two witnesses of " Apocalypse ", the Sunderers of " Last Poems " ; the day of judgment is here which St. John foretold [1] when he saw

> The carnival within our gates,
> Your bodies kicked about the streets.

And in " The Witnesses ", published in Mrs. Monro's

[1] Revelation xi. 8–10.

anthology " Recent Poetry " (1933), Mr. Auden uses the same imagery in describing the death of the ruling classes and suggesting the menace of the future : " Remember the Two ", he admonishes, against the hour

When the green field comes off like a lid
Revealing what were much better hid,
                              unpleasant ;
And look ! behind without a sound
The woods have come up and are standing round
                              in deadly crescent.

And the bolt is sliding in its groove,
Outside the window is the black remov-
                              er's van,
And now with sudden swift emergence
Come the women in dark glasses, the hump-backed surgeons
                              and the scissor-man.

There is never any doubt in his poetry that crisis is at hand.

The obscurity of Mr. Auden's verse, then, is notice-able from the start. But parallel with the involved style of the lyric and reflective poetry there is a straight-forward manner : a manner which, as we have seen, sometimes insists on plainness to the point of truculence. As he turns towards satire he writes more readily in this style ; it is gaining ground in " The Orators " and " New Country ", and in " The Dance of Death " (1933) it is established. This dramatic piece is " a picture of the decline of a class, of how its members dream of a new life, but secretly desire the old, for there is death inside them ". A capitalist chorus revolve about the figure of Death the Dancer ; changing costume and step with the regularity of a Tiller troupe, these class-bound unfortunates clutch at every nostrum —sun-worship, militant nationalism, a return to nature and the " will of the blood ", the mystic abnegation of self and the exploration of a " Reality " beyond the individual. It is a continual process of withdrawal from community : a retreat within the walls of the nation, to the citadel of the self, to the last keep of the eternal Alone. But one by one the nostrums fail : the fugitives are overtaken ; Mr. Auden has apparently renounced even his half-allegiance to Lawrence. The proletarian audience alternately deride and threaten ; the flight to the Absolute itself proved vain, they begin to invade the stage. It is the signal for a new community of speech and action. Capitalist Death turns in upon itself and dies, leaving the accumulated wealth of centuries to the working classes ; and a new protagonist takes the curtain—Karl Marx, attended by two young Communists. From Communism, it seems, we may expect the cure for the neural itch and the distortions of ingrown virginity.

> Youth says the teacher.
> Youth says the bishop.
> Youth says the bumslapper.

Communism says the poet. But it is still rather a get-together party than the stern substitute for religion Russia has held up to us. One doubts if Lenin would have approved.

From the beginning Mr. Auden recognized the poetic problem of his generation as threefold : [1] to solve (a) " the psychological conflict between self as subject and self as object " ; (b) " the ethical conflict : a struggle to reconcile the notion of Pure Art, ' an art completely isolated from everything but its own laws of operation, and the object to be created as such ', with those exigencies which its conditions of existence as a product of a human mind and culture must involve, where the one cannot be ignored nor the other enslaved " ; (c) " the logical conflict, between the denotatory and the connotatory sense of words ". At a first encounter, however, it is not of conflict that we become aware, but of sureness in the handling of contemporary imagery. Mr. Auden manipulates the language of modern industrial life smoothly and without effort. He does not use it in the manner of an earlier generation, to give an effect of harshness and malaise ; nor is he trying to shock his readers.

> Metals run
> Burnished or rusty in the sun
> From town to town,
> And signals all along are down ;
> Yet nothing passes
> But envelopes between these places,
> Snatched at the gate and panting read indoors,
> And first spring flowers arriving smashed,
> Disaster stammered over wires,
> And pity flashed.

---

[1] Preface to " Oxford Poetry ", 1927, by W. H. Auden and Cecil Day Lewis (Basil Blackwell).

Here the images of silent railway and ominous telegram are chosen to suggest ineluctable disaster, the expected fate of a paralysed race ; and the introduction of a conventional " poetic " image, the " first spring flowers ", with its ugly twist, " arriving smashed ", sharpens the impression of terror. But he can use this contemporary diction equally well in treating the established themes of verse :

> The Spring unsettles sleeping partnerships,
> Foundries improve their casting process, shops
> Open a further wing on credit till
> The winter. In summer boys grow tall
> With running races on the froth-wet sand,
> War is declared there, here a treaty signed ;
> Here a scrum breaks up like a bomb, there troops
> Deploy like birds. But proudest into traps
> Have fallen. These gears which ran in oil for week
> By week, needing no look, now will not work ;
> Those manors mortgaged twice to pay for love
> Go to another.

The stir of spring, the advance of seasons and events, and, in bitter contrast, the retreat of prosperity—to these familiar motives we are compelled, by language commonplace in its own setting but foreign in poetry, to give renewed consideration. This is not the usual vulgar attempt to attract attention by the use of incongruous terms. The imagery is not forced ; in its context it is part of a harmonious unity. Foundries, gears, casting process become as much the material of poetry as the stars and skylarks of the Romantics.

Industrial imagery and terminology are common in

the " Poems ", though they are not always used to such good effect. Dawn is heralded by " the pushing over of important levers " ; a solitary truck speaks of autumn and the last of shunting ; the Enemy gives warning of his advance by " smokeless chimneys " and unbuilt bridges, by " silted harbours, derelict works ", by

Power stations locked, deserted, since they drew the boiler fires ;
Pylons fallen or subsiding, trailing dead high-tension wires ;

But Mr. Auden draws from other sources as well. The subjects of " Paid on Both Sides " and " Journal of an Airman " demand military terms ; these, however, are found in the poems and throughout " The Orators ". The poet takes up a belligerent attitude in face of crisis ; the heroes of his verse are airmen, spies, doomed fighters. Even his pupils are called as recruits :

You've a very full programme, first aid, gunnery, tactics,
The technique to master of raids and hand-to-hand fighting ;
              Are you in training ?
Are you taking care of yourself ? are you sure of passing
              The endurance test ?

Binoculars and rifle sights, ambushes and parades—the jargon of the O.T.C. is used to emphasize the desperateness of the situation ; quiet sectors are dangerous, loiterers may be shot without warning : the attack is ordered. Military phrases lend plausibility to Mr. Auden's warnings. But their repetition gives the reader an uneasy feeling of enslavement to the standards of force and noise. The poet is not merely writing down to his public. At times he seems never to have escaped

186

from the preoccupations of a boy scout ; we might be
reading Kipling. And this moral toughness often produces a kind of Philistinism, almost a contempt for the
medium he is using ; a Philistinism which expresses
itself, as with Lawrence's later work, in crude satire ;
hence the doggerel of his call to a lost generation :

If we really want to live, we'd better start at once to try ;
If we don't, it doesn't matter, but we'd better start to die.—

and the street-corner oratory of

'Strewth, says I,
They're most of them dummies who want their mummies,
In Rolls or on bicycle they bolt for mama,
Let them scorch as they like for they won't get far.
Look at them now,
Sooner or later it'll come to the pater,
Sooner or later there'll be a row.

The ethical conflict between the " notion of Pure Art "
and " those exigencies which its conditions of existence
as a product of a human mind and culture must involve "
is leaving its trace on his work. We are made witnesses
of a dispute between the lyric and dramatic impulses
from which spring the best of his verse and a satiric
talent which, proceeding from moral reactions, pays no
respect to the traditional dignity of poetry.

   Like Mr. Eliot and Mr. Pound, Mr. Auden often
focuses our attention by particularizing his images.
The Enemy on the frontier hold, not simply a fort,
but a " squat Pictish tower " ; the area between the
lines is not merely closed :

There's no fire in the waiting-room now at the climbers'
    Junction,
            And all this year
Work has been stopped on the power-house ; the wind
    whistles under
            The half-built culverts.

Metaphorical passages are given actuality by the introduction of concrete illustrations : they are given, too,
a dramatic quality. For with Mr. Auden metaphor and
symbol are frequently less decorative than dramatic ;
they are employed, not to extend an idea, but to advance
the action displayed or implicit in much of his best work.

> We have brought you, they said, a map of the country ;
> Here is the line that runs to the vats,
> This patch of green on the left is the wood,
> We've pencilled an arrow to point out the bay.
> No thank you, no tea ; why look at the clock.
> Keep it ? Of course. It goes with our love.

Here the first verse gives out the component symbols
of a poem : country, vats, wood, bay, clock, love. In
this simple statement is the germ of action ; not the
character addressed, but the symbols are to be the pro-
tagonists. In the second verse the same line-endings
are used in a different sequence : [1]

> We shall watch your future and send our love.
> We lived for years, you know, in the country,
> Remember at week-ends to wind up the clock.
> We've wired to our manager at the vats.
> The tides are perfectly safe in the bay
> But whatever you do don't go to the wood.

---

[1] Possibly imitated from Mr. Day Lewis : cf. p. 202.

They are transposed in each succeeding verse. And
as their order changes their part in the action changes ;
clock turns from safeguard to fetter, the prohibited wood
becomes a source of fresh life, love, from passive grown
active, points to a new country. The poem is an attack
on habit and docility. That attack is immeasurably
strengthened by the dramatic use of plain symbols and
by the stylistic criticism of *cliché* implied in the union
of repetition with a constantly revolving sequence.

We have seen that the process of particularization is
sometimes carried too far ; the image, the allusion,
becomes not merely particular but also private ; it
becomes, in fact, so particular that possibly only Mr·
Auden can understand it. But the obscurity of much
of his verse has other sources. It is due, as I have said,
partly to the suppression of links in the thought. And
to the difficulties of an incompletely logical sequence
of ideas are added the difficulties of syntax. " Paid on
Both Sides " opens with a short prose passage in which
the omission of definite article, and even of the subject
of a sentence, gives the narrative an air of breathless-
ness. This sets the pace for the whole play, which
moves with gathering speed to disaster ; and throughout we find fragments of verse and prose clipped to the
bare essentials. Mr. Auden's most difficult pieces are
often difficult largely as a result of work-paring. And
together with compression and elision we find inver-
sion : " Our maddened set we foot " ;

> Expect we routed shall
> Upon your peace ;

And sometimes the syntax breaks all the rules at once :

> These nissen huts if hiding could
> Your eye inseeing from
> Firm fenders were, but look ! to us
> Your loosened angers come.

The Ode in which these phrases occur has, probably with intention, the rhythm of an Ancient and Modern hymn ; it has also an air of archaism. Here and there in the verse we find evidence for the influence of early English epic poetry ; partly in a mood of toughness and endurance :

> None knows of the next day if it be less or more, the sorrow :
> Escaping cannot try ;
> Must wait though it destroy.

—more noticeably in the technique. In the " Poems ", and increasingly in " The Orators ", alliteration is used in the Anglo-Saxon manner ; the Observer of the Airman's alphabet, for instance, is described as

> Peeper through periscope
> and peerer at pasture
> and eye in the air.

Sometimes the movement and texture of the verse is influenced by Gerard Manley Hopkins ; in " New Country " we find—

> Me, March, you do with your movements master and rock
> With wing-whirl, whale-wallow, silent budding of cell ;

Throughout alliteration is handled with facility and

exuberance. Another feature of the technique is the use of dissonance—a legacy, possibly, from Wilfred Owen. It is found in line-endings : sometimes in conjunction with rhyme, more often alone ; occasionally within the line :

> " O do you imagine," said fearer to farer,
> " That dusk will delay on your path to the pass,
> Your diligent looking discover the lacking
> Your footsteps feel from granite to grass ? "

And it is used to brilliant effect. Mr. Auden can impart to the short line the droop of fatigue :

> Hear last in corner
> The pffwungg of burner
> Accepting dearth
> The shadow of death.

Or he can give the iambic pentameter the rhythm and cadence of despair (witness the passage quoted on p. 185) ; or even infuse a kind of grandeur into the moral exhortation :

> Publish each healer that in city lives
> Or country houses at the end of drives ;
> Harrow the house of the dead ; look shining at
> New styles of architecture, a change of heart.

His facility in verse is prodigious. His work has variety of metrical scheme ; command of rhythm ; a mastery of texture which amounts to virtuosity. He handles assonance and dissonance, rhymeless verse and rhym-

O

ing. And he has the rare ability to control the long line, to climb from the murk of

> Doom is dark and deeper than any sea-dingle.—

to the brilliant

> Lucky with day approaching, with leaning dawn.

At his worst he never quite loses the sense of movement. Lawrence towards the end of his life would slip sulkily into the rhythms of speech ; Mr. Auden, following him, still retains the rhythms of verse.

But facility is sometimes a stumbling-block. He can write in the manner of a hymn or of " Locksley Hall " [1] ; he can imitate Hopkins or the early English epic ; tub-thumping and the grand-manner are both within his range ; not surprising that he grows careless. We have seen how moral reactions and public school boisterous-ness combine to produce doggerel ; even in careful reflective verse there is occasionally a tendency to the slipshod perilously near vulgarity. In " The Dance of Death " he has relied too much on his facility. The piece was apparently intended not for publication but for performance ; the fact remains that it was written : that it was published : that it is offered for critical consideration. Its main interest lies in its attempt to put the *revue* manner to serious use ; it is a development of the form used by Mr. Eliot in " Sweeney Agonistes ". Mr. Auden uses, in his attack on the past, imitations

---

[1] E.g. the passage quoted on p. 186. Cf. " Poetry Direct and Oblique ", by E. M. W. Tillyard, p. 193 (Chatto & Windus).

of popular songs—the music-hall narrative, the martial
chorus, the jazz ditty ; he uses, too, such features of
modern civilization as Announcer and microphone.
The play has energy and unity of movement. But the
verse is shoddy ; it takes on too accurately the characteristics of what it burlesques. " The Dance of
Death " is an illustration of his capacity for exercising
his talent in a variety of mediums. But it shows no
technical advance ; and from the psychological point
of view it does no more than confirm the indications
of belief given in earlier work.

We see, then, in Mr. Auden an uncommon talent,
but a talent as yet uncertain of its direction. The
satiric and the lyric impulses are constantly at war in
his poetry ; the satiric tending to express itself in verse
of a bellicose directness, the lyric inclining to obscurity
and involution. The dispute is echoed in the division
between the personal and the impersonal poetry ; Mr.
Auden allows the one to overlap the province of the
other but fails to make a synthesis of the two. Stronger
than the satiric or the lyric impulse, and permeating
both the private and the public verse, is a dramatic
quality : the quality which gives movement to moral
exhortation, speed to narrative ; which redeems doggerel from dulness ; which adds suspense to warnings
of crisis :

> In sanatoriums they laugh less and less,
> Less certain of cure ; and the loud madman
> Sinks now into a more terrible calm.

But parallel with the dispute between satiric and lyric,

between impersonal and private poetry is a third conflict which sometimes threatens to vitiate even the dramatic impulse. Not the "psychological conflict between self as subject and self as object", not "the logical conflict between the denotatory and the connotatory sense of words" of which he speaks in his statement of the threefold poetic problem ; Mr. Auden is not noticeably disquieted by these. The ethical conflict it is which conditions his poetry. We have seen how moral preoccupations assert themselves, how his verse becomes more and more overtly the manifesto of a political belief. It is a belief without claims to orthodoxy even within its own limits ; nevertheless it makes on his work the demands of a creed backed by authority. And the conflict resolves itself into a battle between art and propaganda—a propaganda which denies poetry the right to obey its own laws and submit to its own logic. To reconcile the two—this is the problem which faces him. There are times when defeat seems imminent, when poetry seems on the verge of enslavement. But there is in his talent a toughness amounting at times almost to brutality. This, while it frees his poetry from self-regard, may also serve as a defence against too uncritical a submergence in an idea. Meanwhile it accords with the temper of his generation ; and it strengthens in his work that true contemporaneity which is always innate, never acquired.

. . . .

I have discussed the poetry of Mr. Auden in some detail because he seems to me the most individual and influential of the new generation. The work of Mr. Day Lewis shows a talent less self-willed, less boisterous, less robust ; a talent which, left to itself, might even have kept aloof from politics. In 1927 Mr. Day Lewis was co-editor with Mr. Auden of " Oxford Poetry ". Two years earlier " Beechen Vigil ", his first book of verse, had been published ; but there was nothing to warn us of what was ahead ; here was a collection of amiably adolescent verse with which we need not now concern ourselves. " Country Comets " (1928) was more solid ; but it was not until " Transitional Poem " (1929) that his work demanded serious critical consideration.

The book was still adolescent but less amiable. Its writer was in the agreeable and exciting condition of finding his own psychology of supreme interest. The theme of the series of poems which it contains is the transition from confusion to order and certainty, from neutrality and doubt to single-mindedness. The movement is divided into four phases. Firstly, there is the struggle for single-mindedness in the " metaphysical " sphere ; recognition of the need for facing the eternal problems ; dismay at their immensity ; resolution to reconcile the conflict of flesh and spirit, love and time ; acceptance of language as the poet's only defence against the void of doubt and annihilation. Secondly, the " ethical " phase. The writer recalls the heroes of his adolescence and the birth of ambition—ambition which he is for a time tempted to reject in favour of a life of rustic ease. Vainly ; ambition must be faced, not fled ; and he returns to the search for the integral mind, the mind untroubled by the lies and treacheries of physical desire. But physical desire it is which conditions the third, the " psychological " phase. Passion exacts a surrender but does not engulf ; rather it disciplines, driving the lover out of his barren solitude and convincing him that integrity lies within diversity and is won by contact with it ; to be single the mind must reach equilibrium between love and hate. The progress, we see, is a progress inwards ; a movement from the universal questions, through the problems of immediate surroundings, to the riddles of the emotions. It is not, however, as in " The Dance of Death ", a retreat, but an advance through narrowing defiles ; and in Part IV Mr. Day Lewis attempts to relate " the poetic impulse " with the sum of his experience as described in the previous parts. The period of transition is past ; no longer set flatteringly apart from common reality, the poet recognizes that art is not born of self-conscious isolation. It is his business to create poetry from his experience ; it is the business of poetry to act as a burning-glass, to intensify experience. Trial is over ; now for the event.

The significance of the individual poems in the series is elucidated with difficulty : in " Transitional Poem " Mr. Day Lewis insists on obscurity. When discovered it often turns out to be commonplace. I have been compelled in the analysis above to use important words, to talk of annihilation, immensity, the eternal problems. But his reaction to the eternal problems is unimportant.

The interest of the sequence lies, not in its ideas (though these have a psychological importance in view of the later development), but in its poetic vitality, its technical accomplishment, its vigour of phrasing. The metrical forms are mostly of traditional origin, but used with modern freedom. There are rhyming stanzas of from four to eight lines ; blank verse ; decasyllabic couplets ; trimeters, tetrameters, pentameters in successful association :

> So he, who learns to comprehend
> The form of things, will find
> They in his eye that purest star have sown
> And changed his mind to singular stone.

The rhymes are generally orthodox, but we find isolated examples of assonance and dissonance : systems—pistons, reason—poison, cattle—metal. These half rhymes, however, are not used purposively, as in Mr. Auden's poems, where they heighten the melancholy or sharpen the seriousness of a conventional sentiment ; they occur haphazard as if through indolence. More interesting is the range of metaphor. Mr. Day Lewis asserts his contemporaneity by drawing on the resources of science and industry. The lover travels " a loopline " ; soul has its " ektogenesis," life its

> . . . pistons
> Pounding into their secret cylinder

Or there is the wireless metaphor ; or the mining metaphor—" the golden seams that cram the night " ; and a whole series of electrical metaphors. Love has

197

" terminals ", desire " charged batteries ", flesh and
spirit are

> Twin poles energic, they
> Stand fast and generate
> This spark that crackles in the void
> As between fate and fate.

The allusions of the poem are less up to date—for
Mr. Day Lewis is sufficiently under the influence of
Mr. Eliot to make allusions and supply references.
Here are the old classical favourites—Artemis, Minos,
Helen, Nestor, Priapus, Scamander, Cronos ; we are
referred also to Donne, Dante, Spinoza, Henry James
and Miss Sophie Tucker.   He has even been reading
the Old Testament, if we are to judge by the mention
of Abraham, Adam, Agag, Ararat, the Ark, Leviathan,
Babel and Sheba.   " Transitional Poem " shows its
author still impressed by his elders : by traditional
meditative poetry ; by Mr. Eliot ; even by Mr. Humbert Wolfe,[1] whose echo may be detected in such lines as

> These, then, have my allegiance ; they whose shining
> Convicted my false dawn of flagrant night,
> Yet ushered up the sun, as poets leaning
> Upon a straw surmise the infinite.

But he is reaching out towards an individual imagery.
In his next book we see the escape from adolescent
egotism and the further movement towards contemporary expression.

   " From Feathers to Iron " was published in 1931.

[1] " Country Comets " is strongly influenced by Mr. Wolfe.

The title is exact ; this is indeed a progress from fly-
away indecision to metal resolution. Mr. Day Lewis
even congratulates himself a little too much on his
new heavy-weight responsibilities. Feathers stand for
flowering passion, iron for passion bearing, not flowers,
but fruit ; the poet assumes paternity. The cycle opens
with an assertion of love's self-sufficiency. Passion's
kingdom is mapped out ; there remains to

> Plough up the meadowland, reclaim the marshes.

The lovers abandon town for the autumnal country-side,
resolved not to " insulate " their " strong currents of
ecstasy " but to " breed units of power " ; the

> Terminus where all feather joys alight

is before them. Pregnancy brings fear and hope ;
spring bears the reminder that death as well as birth
is " coiled in our bones ". They " seek a new world
through old workings " ; but pain is needed to " blast
the sharp scarps ". The unborn child may make peace
in the soul's division, grow up a new " white hope "
for society ; but what of destiny and the perfidies
awaiting eagerness and innocence ? The first fire of
passion has been extinguished ;

> Do not expect again a phoenix hour,
> The triple-towered sky, the dove complaining,
> Sudden the rain of gold and heart's first ease
> Tranced under trees by the eldritch light of sundown.

—to what end ? That an heir may inherit disintegration, " Worn-out machinery, an exhausted farm " ?

Pride reasserts itself; constancy takes firmer root. There is a moment of terror as crisis approaches; then an outburst of joy. A son is born; or, as Mr. Day Lewis puts it,

Early this morning whistle in the cutting told
Train was arriving, hours overdue, delayed
By snow-drifts, engine-trouble, Act of God, who cares now?

Even obstetrics are mechanized.

The Epilogue expresses a different mood; there is a move away from the personal. It is addressed to Mr. Auden, to whom it offers homage:

But I, who saw the sapling, prophesied
A growth superlative and branches writing
On heaven a new signature.

Homage and allegiance; suddenly Mr. Day Lewis pledges himself to the march on an unknown future preached in the Auden " Poems ". It is a desperate measure:

Say that a rescue party should see fit
To do us some honour, publish our diaries,
Send home the relics—how should we thank them?

But the writer has been convinced of its necessity. And he has found, as we shall see, an influence to which he can submit whole-heartedly.

The fragments quoted show that he has developed his bent for contemporary imagery. Certain metaphors he shares with Mr. Auden, to whom we possibly owe the recurrent railway and aeronautic images, some of the industrial symbols and a few military and athletic ones. I have cited images drawn from agriculture, mining and electrical science ; and we find, too, metaphors inspired by astronomy and photography, and such machine-age words as " turbine ", " tractor ", " grain-elevator ", " arc-lamp ", " multi-engined ". There are, it is true, conventional " poetic " images : music, the lark, sunset, stars, dawn. But often these are used as a foil to the industrial image ; willowherb glows on a slagheap, spring is double-faced :

> Look there, gasometer rises,
> And here bough swells to bud.

The advance into contemporaneity, however, does not mean an advance into involution. The poem is less difficult than " Transitional Poem ", and certainly less difficult than Mr. Auden's work ; it has only rare obscurities. But that Mr. Day Lewis is following Mr. Auden is clear, not only from the declared faith of the Epilogue, but also from the technique of " From Feathers to Iron ". We find dissonance purposely used in the Auden manner : living—retrieving, knowing—renewing. Or we come across a passage of Audenesque alliteration :

> Like Jesuits in jungle we journey
> Deliberately bearing to brutish tribes
> Christ's assurance, arts of agriculture.

And it is even possible to discover a fragment of Audenesque lopped and elided syntax.

The metrical forms are related to those of " Transitional Poem " ; once more the sequence is written for the most part in rhymed stanzas, which now show greater assurance in handling. He has become a competent technician ; and when he experiments, producing pairs of verses with identical line-endings,[1] the experiment is successful enough not to obtrude. One poem, written in irregular unrhymed verse, is still influenced by Mr. Eliot ; it is full of echoes of " Ash Wednesday ", " Animula " and " The Waste Land ". But the introduction of an altered Phlebas passage provides one of the few allusions in the book. Mr. Day Lewis no longer cites the classics or the Bible ; nowadays it is the trade depression or the theory of aeronautics that is cited. The book is throughout unmistakably contemporary. Yet it does not display the contempt for literature as we know it which characterizes much modern verse. He draws for his diction on sources unknown to an earlier generation. But in his employment of them he does not differ from his predecessors. Often a metaphor is sustained throughout a poem in the manner of seventeenth-century metaphysical verse ; often he handles his imagery with conscious pleasure in decoration. In " From Feathers to Iron " he is still writing " poetic " verse. As such it has the qualities of passion, energy, precision. At this point of time, however, it possesses for us another interest. The subject is universal ; the mood has little that is essentially modern. But the whole poem has been re-

[1] Cf. p. 188.

vitalized by its imagery ; this and nothing else gives it contemporaneity. It is not a forced contemporaneity ; barring occasional extravagances and, now and then, a false note, the diction proceeds from a conviction of its fitness. And from the conflict between human theme and inhuman imagery emerges a poetry often harsh, sometimes brutal, which nevertheless persists in being alive.

" Transitional Poem " showed us a young man struggling to break out of adolescent isolation ; in " From Feathers to Iron " we watch him undergoing a serious emotional experience and through it growing aware of a responsibility for society in general. With " The Magnetic Mountain " (1933) the emancipation from autobiography is complete ; now we see where the faith pledged in the Epilogue is leading. The influence of Mr. Auden on " From Feathers to Iron " is, as we have seen, mainly technical ; it produces certain tricks of style and urges in the direction of a greater modernity of phrase. In " The Magnetic Mountain " Mr. Day Lewis has made a complete surrender. The themes are pure Auden : warnings against the Enemy, threats of disaster, promises of salvation through " the attacking movement ". The end of the traditional track has been reached, he says ; before the start for Terra Incognita, the Magnetic Mountain, let us make a tour of inspection through the past. And he sets himself to arraign the defendants,[1] indict the enemies who enforced the old

[1] For the plan of Parts 2 and 3, cf. Mr. Humbert Wolfe's " Requiem " (Benn).

order.   Parenthood unwilling to renounce its possessive-
ness ; education inoculating against

The infection of faith and the excess of life.

time-serving religion ; love seeking to confine the
integral spirit—one by one the defendants speak and
are answered.   One by one the enemies are condemned :
the siren of sex ; the cheating press ; the substitute-
religions of science ; the false dreams of irresponsible
idealism.   And so he turns his back on the past :
" zero hour is signalled ".   It is a summons to attack
fear, hypocrisy, decaying tradition,

> Hard Cheese the Confidence-Tricker,
> Private Loot, General Pride,
> And Lust the sultry-eyed.

And the objective is

> . . . a world where the will of all shall be raised to highest
>   power,
> Village or factory shall form the unit.
> Control shall be from the centres, quick brain, warm heart,
> And the bearings bathed in a pure
> Fluid of sympathy.   There possession no more shall be part
> Of the man, where riches and sacrifice
> Are of flesh and blood, sex, muscles, limbs and eyes.
> Each shall give of his best.   It shall seem proper
> For all to share what all produced.

Already we pull up at a form of communism : a communism modified by the Lawrentian creed.

The technique of the poem is more imitative than
that of " From Feathers to Iron ".   Alliteration is

gaining ground—" Counters of spoons and content with cushions " : " no wing-room for Wystan " :

> Foam-stepper, star-steerer, freighter and fighter—

Dissonance, grown frequent enough to be no longer noticeable, is used not only in line-endings but also within the line :

> Simple that world, of two dimensions,
> Of stone mansions and good examples ;

Interest in technique is marked throughout ; the patterns of rhyme and dissonance are more elaborate ; the metrical forms, though often similar to those of earlier work, incline to greater complexity without loss of discipline. The imagery develops on the lines of " From Feathers to Iron ". It is a " light engine " that Mr. Day Lewis takes for his last excursion into the past, " a cantilever bridge " that must be built over chaos ; for the coming revolution volunteers are wanted

> To go aloft and cut away tangled gear ;
> Break through to blocked galleries below pit-head,
> Get in touch with living and raise from the dead :
> Men to catch spies, fly aeroplanes,
> Harrow derelict acres and mend the drains.

Once more there are military and athletic metaphors ; images drawn from electrical science, navigation, aeronautics, engineering ; the terminology of agriculture and industry. But the imagery no longer has the spontaneity of "From Feathers to Iron " : we no longer experience the shock of surprise and pleasure at the successful union of emotional theme and unemotional phrase. Mr. Auden's influence has falsified the tone of Mr. Day Lewis's work ; the flat or jeering statement which is often effective in " The Orators " seems forced in " The Magnetic Mountain ". For it is not only by subject matter, by tricks of technique, by a certain roughening of imagery that we are reminded of the allegiance ; the mood of the poem is derivative.

Look west, Wystan, lone flyer, birdman, my bully boy !

—the invocation of his leader shows that a new kind of excitement possesses his verse. It is the excitement of community of action.

Wystan, Rex, all of you that have not fled,

—the repetition of Christian names emphasizes the solidarity of the group. The action is primarily not literary, but social, though a literary movement keeps pace with the political movement. And it is an action, so it seems, against desperate odds : against the massed resources of authority, falsehood, lethargy. Consciousness of isolation in community magnifies the figures of the opposition ; Mr. Day Lewis follows Mr. Auden in personifying moral qualities, in lending to " Private Loot ", " General Pride ", " Sir Après-moi-le-déluge " the stature of a Goliath. It also generates a kind of arrogance in the isolated ; poetry becomes the last

206

message of the saved to the lost. Or of games master to under-developed pupil. The men of the future will be

Bright of eye, champions for speed,
They sing their own songs, they are active, they play not
    watch :
Happy at night talking
Of the demon bowler cracked over the elm-trees,
The reverse pass that won the match.

This is not metaphor : Mr. Day Lewis has accepted muscular morality. He has gone out gospel-riding with Mr. Auden. And on the way he has learned something of the truculent attitude towards literature of his companion.

    Children of the sahib, the flag and the mater,
    Grim on golf-courses and haggard on horses
    They try to live but they've ceased to matter :

Technical virtuosity becomes a matter of mere bravado —or of advertisement. It is the drum beaten outside the gospeller's tent.

 The poet, then, has emerged from his personal pre-occupations and advanced into the world of practical affairs. It is a movement of expansion—the reverse of that described in the first three sections of " Transitional Poem " ; and it is the logical outcome of the effort to escape from the self promised in the fourth section. But he has failed to co-ordinate the " poetic impulse " with his new experience. Mr. Day Lewis was associated with Mr. Auden in the statement of the threefold poetic problem ; and, like Mr. Auden, he has been for the moment defeated by the ethical conflict. Defeated, rather, by the ethical conflict and by Mr. Auden. A natural vitality has been induced to outrun its strength ; an impulse towards decoration has been driven into wrong channels. Mr. Day Lewis's talent inclines towards refined and elaborate phrasing and a certain self-indulgence in metaphor and imagery. Mr. Auden's call to arms has diverted it towards the jerky mechanical movement, the rough bitter manner ; in a word, towards satire. Mr. Day Lewis has the poetic vigour, but not, I think, the speed requisite for satirical verse ; his later work lacks the readiness, the rapidity which is present even in the crudest of Mr. Auden's burlesques. And the demands of the new creed of belligerence and community of action have transformed his pleasure in decoration ; what at the worst might become a pardonable poetic extravagance, now inclines to vulgarity and noise ; he squanders his imagery. But enough of the original impulse remains unvitiated to prove that he has a genuine talent. Up to now a small talent. But a talent supported by energy and a kind of recklessness which, except in the work of Lawrence, has long been wanting in English poetry.

．　　．　　．　　．　　．　　．　　．

The work of Mr. Stephen Spender aroused interest from its first appearance in 1930, with " Twenty Poems " ; since the publication of " Poems " (1933), in which eleven of the earlier pieces are reprinted, its reputation has steadily grown. Its very differences from the poetry of Mr. Auden and Mr. Day Lewis partly account for its success. It is rarely obscure. It has none of the truculence, none of the harsh jeering quality of Mr. Auden's work ; it does not indulge in the semi-philosophical reflections which intimidate readers of Mr. Day Lewis's early verse. Its imagery is not obtrusively contemporary ; Mr. Spender does not translate every idea into terms of the hangar or the power station. At a first glance, indeed, his work appears far less experimental than that of the two writers discussed above. It seems gentler, smoother, more " poetic " ; the reader bred in the tradition of romantic poetry feels that here is the kind of literature he knows.

Like Mr. Auden and Mr. Day Lewis, Mr. Spender writes on personal as well as on impersonal themes, on the memory of love as well as on the promise of revolution. The impulse towards the expression of personal emotion is strong ; and the verse which results from it has a directness and a simplicity rare in modern poetry. Mr. Spender describes the desolation of an untenanted room :

> Oh empty walls, book-carcases, blank chairs
> All splintered in my head and cried for you.

or emphasizes the association of a scene with a person :

> Till the identification of a morning—
> Expansive sheets of blue rising from fields
> Roaring movements of light observed under shadow—
> With his figure leaning over a map, is now complete.

or contrasts the physical reality of love with its ultimate evasion :

> The promise hangs, this swarm of stars and flowers,
> And then there comes the shutting of a door.

But soon enough we are reminded of modernity. The lost lover, his happiness corrupted, goes back to the " turning of bolts or driving a machine " ; passion assumes a strength beyond the human :

> I must have love enough to run a factory on,
> Or give a city power, or drive a train.

And invocation of the beloved takes on a rough quality :

> Your games of cards, hockey with toughs,
> Winking at girls, shoes cribbed from toffs,
> Like the encircling summer dew
> Glaze me from head to toe.

The apostles of the new ethics have learnt their lesson from Lawrence ; they rejoice, not in resisting life, but in accepting it ; moral grandeur for them is bound up with the physical, and to express nobility physical praise becomes the most apt :

> Him I delight in accepts joy as joy ;
> He is richened by sorrow as a river by its bends,
> He is the swallower of fire,
> His bowels are molten fire ; when he leaves his friend
> He takes pleasure in icy solitude ; he is the dandy ;
> He is the swimmer, waves only lift him higher,
> He is the rose, sultry loveliness does not oppress him ;
> The clouds of our obscuring disillusion
> Are thoughts which shade his brow, and then he smiles.

Mr. Spender is urged by the lyric impulse, but this is not the poetry to which we have been accustomed. He can, it is true, write conventionally of the " constancy of natural rest ", of evening with the cry of gulls and the " hammering surf ". But suddenly we meet a lyric poetry with a fresh set of motives : a lyric poetry which delights in the air-liner :

> More beautiful and soft than any moth
> With burring furred antennae feeling its huge path
> Through dusk,

in the pylons, mocking the valley's " gilt and evening look " with " the quick perspective of the future " ; in the express plunging through the night :

> Ah, like a comet through flame, she moves entranced
> Wrapt in her music no bird song, no, nor bough
> Breaking with honey buds, shall ever equal.

He uses the contemporary motive with complete confidence in its aptness to poetry. He does not find it necessary to envelope the theme of descending aeroplane or departing train in a false romanticism ; to him the train, the aeroplane has an actual beauty of its own. But it is a beauty which scarcely troubles to conceal a threat. The pylons are " tall with prophecy ", the air-liner crossing the " fraying edge " of industry, passing chimneys and " squat buildings ", nears a deadlier symbol :

> Religion stands, the church blocking the sun.

We begin to see that his feeling for the mechanical image

is partly due to its inclination away from the past. In the last poem of the book it acquires a revolutionary inclination. Too late, he says, for gardens, singing feasts, dreams of suns :

> Instead, watch images of flashing brass
> That strike the outward sense, the polished will
> Flag of our purpose which the wind engraves.

It becomes a moral duty to renounce a soft for a hard beauty, to feed the eye on the strict outline ; thus may the mind learn energy and a will towards change ; thus may it oppose to the guns and battleships of " the antique Satan " a steely purpose :

> Our programme like this, yet opposite,
> Death to the killers, bringing light to life.

We have come to the second impulse which governs his poetry : the impulse towards revolution. He describes in Eliot-like phrases the emotional disintegration of a passing generation : a parent's quarrel overheard by their son :

> " I was awake at three." " I heard the moth
> Breed perilous worms." " I wept
> All night, watching your rest." " I never slept
> Nor sleep at all." Thus ghastly they speak, both.

—or recalls the isolation of a well-to-do child amidst the contemptuous poor :

> They were lithe, they sprang out behind hedges
> Like dogs to bark at our world. They threw mud
> And I looked another way, pretending to smile.
> I longed to forgive them, yet they never smiled,

The will to revolution has not saved him from all knowledge of disillusion, of

> . . . the gradual day
> Weakening the will
> Leaking the brightness away,

But he has turned away from the " brilliance of cities ", from the " streets the rich built ", from the houses designed " to breed money on money " towards " the beautiful generation that shall spring from our sides ". It is time to renounce the dead wealth of the past and to count rather

> . . . those fabulous possessions
> which begin with your body and your fiery soul :—

time to remember " the essential delight of the blood " ; time to honour the truly great :

> . . . those who in their lives fought for life
> Who wore at their hearts the fire's centre.
> Born of the sun they travelled a short while towards the sun,
> And left the vivid air signed with their honour.

Once more we hear the echo of Lawrence, the summons to life. For Mr. Spender it is a choice between life and death.

> And our strength is now the strength of our bones
> Clean and equal like the shine from snow
> And the strength of famine and of our enforced idleness,
> And it is the strength of our love for each other.

The crisis of which Mr. Auden warns us is not merely

at hand ; it is upon us. But Mr. Auden's belligerent purpose is softened here. " Poetry ", says Mr. Spender, " is the language of moments in which we see ourselves or other people in our or their true relation to humanity or to nature. Poetry is certainly ' counter-revolutionary ' in the sense that it contains an element of pity." [1] Pity exists even in the satirical poetry of Mr. Auden and Mr. Day Lewis. But it is a pity approaching patronage ; with Mr. Spender it is pity for a suffering in some way shared :

> . . . at corners of day
> Road drills explore new areas of pain,
> Nor summer nor light may reach down here to play.
> The city builds its horror in my brain,
> This writing is my only wings away.

Let us make no mistake—he does not accept the proffered means of escape. To the revolutionary, he says in the essay quoted above, poetry is an idealist drug ; that is to say, it enables the writer to evade social problems and solace himself in a world of the imagination. But it is the duty of the poet with communist sympathies, resisting the enticements of practical politics, to persist in his poetry. Without any attempt at propaganda art is capable of communicating " the elements of disruption " latent in society ; it can " make clear to the practical revolutionaries the historic issues which are in the deepest sense political ". Mr. Spender shirks neither art nor politics ; it is his endeavour by stating " the causes of our present frustration " to

[1] " New Country ", p. 69 (Hogarth Press).

214

" prepare the way for a new kind of society ". And so he points without comment to the seaport with on the one hand its maze of streets, its prostitutes, its " flaring caves ", on the other the quarter of the merchants, " well-fed, well-lit, well-spoken ". Or he shows us the bitter leisure of the unemployed :

> They lounge at corners of the street
> And greet friends with a shrug of shoulder
> And turn their empty pockets ᴐut,
> The cynical gestures of the poor.

—or depicts a resignation beyond the reach of hope :

> They raise no hands, which rest upon their knees,
> But lean their solid eyes against the night,
> Dimly they feel
> Only the furniture they use in cells.

Clearly he is using poetry for the ends of propaganda ; this is a purposive communication of the " elements of disruption ". But art is not enslaved. And even when the theme is repellent, even when he is advancing the anti-individualist doctrines which are the least palatable of the communist faith, the feeling for poetry is not wholly submerged. " The Funeral " records the death of a unit in the world state who " excelled all others in making driving belts ", and the reactions of his fellows.

They think how one life hums, revolves and toils,
One cog in a golden and singing hive :
Like spark from fire, its task happily achieved,
It falls away quietly.

No more are they haunted by the individual grief
Nor the crocodile tears of European genius,
The decline of a culture
Mourned by scholars who dream of the ghosts of Greek boys.

Nothing can disguise the false psychology of this passage, nothing mitigate its facile optimism. As logic it is immediately rejected ; but as poetry it retains a certain plausibility.

Propaganda, then, is not an uneasy element in his verse, though we are constantly made aware of its presence. Of technique we are less conscious ; Mr. Spender has none of the stylistic peculiarities which characterize the work of Mr. Auden and Mr. Day Lewis. Dissonance is scarcely used ; alliteration occurs only in isolated examples :

> sparkling on waves and spangled under trees

The syntax is generally orthodox. And the metrical schemes, though they have an air of freedom, are not obtrusively experimental. Mr. Spender readily handles rhyme ; he even uses such a traditional form as the sonnet. The unrhymed verse moves smoothly and steadily : it never breaks into the cantering motion of Mr. Auden's satirical mood. Even his imagery has as much in common with romantic poetry as with the new movement towards the mechanical, the contemporary. The march of pylons " dwarfs our emerald country " ; but it is a march towards cities

> Where often clouds shall lean their swan-white neck.

To-day we watch " the failure of banks " ; but those who follow us shall see

> . . . the admiring dawn explode like a shell
> Around us, dazing us with its light like snow.

Love may be compared with the power which runs a factory or drives a train ; but it is also " formed with the hills " ; it is a " mystery shadowed on the desert floor " ; it is a " swarm of stars and flowers ". Mr. Spender admits the fine phrase, the deliberate " poetic " climax ; illusion dangles before him

> Like the created poem
> Or the dazzling crystal.

In the nine new pieces included in the second edition of the " Poems " (1934) we see, it is true, a kind of hardening of the verse. The themes are similar : memories of private emotion ; regret for the ideal self

> Whose adored desire was to die for the world.—

hope for a new world that shall effect its beauty " without robbery ". But the expression of private emotion is a shade sharper ; regret has lost its first directness and learned involution ; hope itself has acquired toughness by acquaintance with doubt, the eternal Perhaps —doubt even of revolution, like Leviathan

> hugely nosing at edge of antarctic ?

A certain tightening of technique is shown by comparison of the poem " Van der Lubbe " published in

" The Spectator " (September 29, 1933) with the version in the second edition of the " Poems ". But Mr. Spender is still moving along the lines marked out in his earliest published work ; there is no repression of a native impulse, no submission to an alien influence comparable with that made by Mr. Day Lewis in " The Magnetic Mountain ".

Conformity with the popular conception of poetry makes his work more generally acceptable than that of Mr. Auden or Mr. Day Lewis ; lyric, after all, arouses a readier response than satirical verse. He achieves, too, a better synthesis than either Mr. Auden or Mr. Day Lewis between propaganda and art. The conflict in his work as a whole between the personal and the impersonal is startling enough. We have only to compare the love poetry with such a piece as " The Funeral " to see how sharply his mind is divided. But in the individual poems conflict is resolved ; the ethical problem is mastered. Within its limits his verse is more accomplished, more complete than Mr. Auden's. It is more accomplished because its range is smaller, completer because it is aware of fewer possibilities. Like Mr. Day Lewis's, in fact, it is so far a minor talent ; Mr. Auden's may become a major talent.

. . . .

Obviously we cannot make a final critical judgment of a poet at the outset of his career ; and with the three writers here discussed it is not possible to do much more than indicate the themes of their verse and their manner of treatment. But in doing this we become aware of a community of aim between the most dissimilar talents : we become aware of a new mood in poetry. The despair of an earlier generation has been discarded in favour of passionate hope ; negation has been turned to affirmation. Poetry remains hostile to the society in which it finds itself. But it no longer looks, for a solution of its problems, away from the civilization with which it is at war. There is, as we have seen, a romantic impulse in the poetry of Miss Sitwell, an impulse which emerges, too, with Mr. Sassoon ; we do not expect to find it in the work of Lawrence or Mr. Eliot. Yet in the violence of their reactions to modern civilization we may still see romanticism at work. Romantic poetry —the work of Keats and Shelley in particular—was responsible for the tradition of the poet's unbearable sensibility in contact with society. It was not generally accepted before the nineteenth century : to-day it is rejected again. Lawrence, Mr. Eliot, Miss Sitwell, Mr. Sassoon are romantics in so far as they allow themselves to be tortured by society. Now a new toughness has come into being which refuses to be tormented. Poetry suddenly announces that its own problem is to a certain extent identical with that of humanity at large, and to that extent can be solved by practical politics. There must be no surrender to suffering ; certainly none to the irrational.

In this new poetry we see the union of two influences —the influence of Lawrence, the influence of Mr. Eliot. I have tried to show how strongly the younger generation of writers is imbued with Lawrence's idea of new life. But Lawrence always held to his belief in aristocracy; an aristocracy based, not on wealth or birth, but on nobility of being. His followers have given the creed a political bias. There must indeed be new life within the individual; but the emphasis is on new life within society, a new principle of equality; the communist paradox insists that all men are aristocrats. It is difficult to imagine a more striking reversal from the mood of Mr. Eliot's verse, from his appeal to a small and highly educated section of the public; though critics who complain that his is a class poetry must remember that Mr. Auden and Mr. Day Lewis too are moving in the direction of a class poetry, and that Mr. Spender looks forward [1] to the development of a purely proletarian literature. Yet without the work of Mr. Eliot the recent movements in poetry would not have been possible. The new generation have rejected his mood of disillusion and that part of his material which seems to them literary and therefore dead. His contribution to the manner of poetry they have not been able to reject. From him they have learnt the strength and sharpness which proceed from the union of serious intention with mocking utterance; they have learnt the value of contrasting the undulating with the flat phrase; they have even been infected with a desire for order and authority. For, as Mr. Day Lewis has pointed out,[2] Communism is as much a champion of authority as the Church, only it is a different kind of authority.

[1] " New Country ", pp. 65–7.   [2] Ibid., p. 29.

Poetry, then, has broken out of the seclusion in which it has lately been clinging precariously to existence, and has plunged once more into the business of life. From this new contact with practical affairs we expect something beyond contemporaneity. The supporters of the new movements are inclined to write as if orientation were everything, as if the poet needed no more than to be " abreast of his own times ".[1] Too much of the vitality which we admire in the younger poets is expended on keeping abreast with the times, too little on keeping abreast with art. Yet from the union of talent and energy a genuine literature promises to emerge : a poetry as yet uncertain, fitful, uncontrolled, but still poetry. For those bred in the tradition of nineteenth-century verse it may not always be easy to recognize as poetry. But at least it must not be ignored. For in it is perhaps the germ of a new mode in literature ; a mode we may dislike but shall be compelled to accept.

[1] " New Signatures ", p. 8.